BOURBON

50 Rousing Recipes for a Classic American Spirit

FRED THOMPSON

The Harvard Common Press
Boston, Massachusetts

IN MEMORY OF MY DAD,
E.M. "TOMMY" THOMPSON, WHO LOVED
HIS JACK DANIEL'S OLD NO. 7.
I MISS YOU.

The Harvard Common Press
535 Albany Street
Boston, Massachusetts 02118
www.harvardcommonpress.com

Printed in China
Printed on acid-free paper

Library of Congress Cataloging-in-Publication Data
Thompson, Fred, 1953-
Bourbon : 50 rousing recipes for a classic American spirit / Fred Thompson.
p. cm.
Includes index.
ISBN 978-1-55832-400-8 (alk. paper)
1. Cocktails. 2. Whiskey. I. Title.
TX951.T48136 2010
641.2'52–dc22
2009027603

Special bulk-order discounts are available on this and other Harvard Common Press
books. Companies and organizations may purchase books for premiums or resale,
or may arrange a custom edition, by contacting the Marketing Director at the
address above.

Book design by Elizabeth Van Itallie
Photography by Brian Hagiwara
Prop & food styling by Bret Baughman

10 9 8 7 6 5 4 3 2

CONTENTS

INTRODUCTION 4

BOURBON BASICS 6

THE CLASSICS 20

UPDATED, NEWFANGLED, AND FULL OF FRUIT 40

PIPING HOT AND ICY 62

BOURBON FOR A CROWD 74

EDIBLE BOURBON 84

MEASUREMENT EQUIVALENTS 93

INDEX 94

INTRODUCTION

**"SIP IT AND DREAM—IT IS A DREAM ITSELF.
SIP IT AND SAY THERE IS NO SOLACE FOR THE SOUL, NO TONIC FOR
THE BODY LIKE OLD BOURBON WHISKEY."**
—J. Soule Smith's "Ode to the Mint Julep," written in the 1890s

Bourbon is truly an American spirit. Only in the limestone rock formations of central Kentucky and north-central Tennessee can the water be thus flavored: As it filters through the stone, it grabs just the right chemical balance to make the distillers' yeast robust and vibrant, which produces the dark-honey-golden fluid. Nirvana. Bourbon, named for Kentucky's old Bourbon County, and its close cousin Tennessee whiskey are related to the whiskey-making business in Ireland and Scotland only by generalities. Corn is the grain of choice for American whiskey, from which either a mash or a sour mash is made to kick off fermentation. But that color and smoky-sweet nose with hints of vanilla, caramel, and clove come from freshly charred white oak barrels and the length of time they are allowed to hold the liquor. In Tennessee, the whiskey takes one more step with a charcoal filtration, which some admirers of a man named Jack Daniel or George Dickel believe smoothes out the flavor.

Bourbon and Tennessee whiskey have strolled out of their Southern heritage and left their spiritual homes of Louisville, Bardstown, and Lynchburg to be enjoyed throughout the country. Like another Southern export, NASCAR, bourbon is exploding in consumption and demand. From New York City's hottest bars and restaurants to the hip Mission District of San Francisco is heard the lament "We can't keep bourbon in stock." Also heard: "Our bourbon cocktail sales are up 30 percent." With the reserve, small-batch, and single-barrel bourbons now becoming "top shelf," there is even more interest in bourbon.

Other factors have also created this demand, according to bartenders around the country—the trend back to classic cocktails and bourbon's appeal with American foods. Barbecue (the noun), one of America's biggest food fascinations, is hard to pair with wine, but the smoky sweetness of bourbon and Tennessee whiskey plays on the palate in an enriching way that blends with rather than disturbs the food's essence. A little bourbon and ginger ale sits communally with fried chicken, too. America's newfound interest in Southern foods makes bourbon and Tennessee whiskey the perfect before, during, and after mealtime beverages. America's "native whiskey" seems to prepare your taste buds for big flavors. It is an outstanding pre-dinner quaff, even when followed by wine.

And can you even imagine listening to the blues with Scotch or vodka? America's signature music certainly deserves America's signature spirit.

Bourbon and Tennessee whiskey have even transcended the borders of our country. In 2007 America's spirits exports topped $1 billion, almost all of that bourbon and Tennessee whiskey. You can easily find Jack Daniel's and Maker's Mark in the grocery stores of Italy. They covet Jack Daniel's in Japan, and it is a welcome gift when doing business there, as I discovered a few years ago while on a consulting job in Tokyo. More than 100 countries import American whiskey, including Great Britain, Canada, Germany, Austra-lia, and Japan. China, Vietnam, Brazil, and the old Eastern Bloc countries are new, fast-growing markets for our whiskey.

With small-batch and single-barrel varieties and the almost cult status of some bourbons, the legend continues to grow. Bourbon and Tennessee whiskey are American stories and spirits that deserve their place on the top shelf of our drinking repertoire.

BOURBON BASICS

I f you definitively know who invented bourbon, then stand behind the last person in line who definitively knows who invented bourbon. Its beginnings seem to have been lost, or at least reworked through oral histories in the 1800s. Bill Samuels, the president of Maker's Mark distillery, considers the story of bourbon as one of a "series of happy accidents," and he's right. Much information is sketchy. Some of its history is probably best forgotten or simply has been forgotten because the subject (and its consumption) does tend to create a hazy memory. Much of this story is factual; much is "based on a true story," as they say in the movies.

A WALK THROUGH HISTORY WITH A JULEP CUP IN HAND

In 1791, the newly formed Congress put a tax on whiskey production to help pay the debts that financed the Revolution. This raised the ire of the Scotch-Irish settlers in western Pennsylvania, which was the hub of whiskey production in America. They refused to pay, and the Whiskey Rebellion of 1791 to 1794 began. It also sounds like the beginning of moonshiners and their opposition to taxes. The uprising was so great that President George Washington had to send in a militia to bring peace. That, he found out, was not an easy task. To save face and avoid further troubles, Washington, himself a large whiskey producer at Mount Vernon, agreed to a deal that Virginia's Patrick Henry proposed. Since Kentucky, west of the Allegheny Mountains and a part of Virginia at the time, was exempt from federal law, an arrangement was made for those who were willing to move there. Years before, then-governor of Virginia Thomas Jefferson had offered settlers 60 acres of land in Kentucky if they would build a permanent home there and raise "native corn." Resurrecting this deal dampened the uprising and allowed Washington to expand population growth into that area.

I have yet to meet a family that could eat 60 acres' worth of corn. It's perishable and was too bulky to transport at that time in history. But if you turn it into whiskey . . . Scotch-Irish immigrants, who were quite adept at distilling, bought in to the plan in droves. So whiskey became a creole of their native ways and our native grain, and bourbon was about to be born.

Most of the settlers set up house close to the land offices that the federal government had established to handle allocation of property. These offices were all located on the Limestone Shelf, a geographic area shaped like the upper half of an hourglass that takes up about 25 percent of today's western Kentucky and 5 percent of Tennessee. The water running through this shelf was and is high in calcium and low in iron, ideal for distilling whiskey and also an excellent drink for raising strong-boned thoroughbred horses. Almost every major bourbon producer in America today distills in the Limestone Shelf.

Okay, so now the fuss over origins begins. The Samuels family claims that they have the oldest family still that has remained in continuous operation, starting in 1783. But they didn't start commercial production until 1840. These are the folks behind Maker's Mark. There was some conjecture put forth by Charles Cowdery in 1996 that the first corn-based Kentucky distillery was actually at Fort Harrod, the first European settlement west of the Allegheny Mountains, around 1774. Evan Williams probably opened the first commercial distillery, on the banks of the Ohio River in Louisville, Kentucky, in 1793.

Having been raised a Southern Baptist, I enjoy this part of the story. A Baptist minister named Elijah Craig, from Georgetown, Kentucky, supplemented his ministry income by being a distiller. Although he is often given credit for creating bourbon, there's no evidence that there was one single inventor. Many people had a hand in helping bourbon evolve into its present form. However, legend goes that Elijah Craig made a stunning discovery that does affect how bourbon is produced in the twenty-first century. In the late eighteenth century, the Natchez Trail from Lexington, Kentucky, to New Orleans was flourishing with the whiskey trade. Each barrel that went downriver was stamped with its county of origin. Reverend Craig, looking for a way to save money, found that instead of buying new barrels, he could use fish barrels for storing whiskey. But to get the fish taste out of the barrels, he would burn and char the insides. His first ex-fish barrels, now charred whiskey barrels stamped with "Bourbon" on the outside, went downriver in the summer, and the trip took some 90 days. What arrived in New Orleans was something completely different from what had been shipped. The charred oak and the shipping time had smoothed out the spirit: It had pulled out the vanilla and caramel essences from the barrel, along with a pleasant, sweet smokiness. Interestingly enough, American white oak is the only wood that produces this effect, and in those days, white oak grew in abundance in Kentucky. Folks in New Orleans went crazy over this new spirit and demanded more of that whiskey from "Bourbon." It is odd that Craig stamped "Bourbon" on his barrels, though, considering he never distilled in nor lived in Bourbon County. Remember, legend is involved in this story.

The year 1795 saw the beginning of a dynasty. Jacob Beam sold his first barrel of "Old Jake Beam Sour." Seven generations of the family have tended over the brand, now known as Jim Beam. Fred Noe is the present keeper of the craft.

The recipe for bourbon continued to be refined, and a huge part of what bourbon is today is credited to either Dr. James C. Crow or Dr. Jason S. Amburgey (depending on whom you talk to), who introduced the sour mash process, in which each new fermentation is conditioned with some of the spent mash from the previous batch. This new process allowed for the mash to control the growth of bacteria that could harm the whiskey and created a proper pH balance for the distilling to take place. Sour mash also helps maintain a consistent quality and taste from batch to batch. By 2005 all straight bourbons were using this sour mash process that was first conceived at the Old Oscar Pepper distillery, which is now the Woodford Reserve Distillery in Woodford County, Kentucky.

The word "bourbon" first showed up on bottle labels around 1840. It's ironic that the Bourbon County stamp on those first barrels made it famous, because the state has drawn and redrawn county lines, and now no distillers that produce bourbon operate within the current boundaries of Bourbon County.

During the Civil War there was a shortage of whiskey. Manpower for the distillers was in short supply, and many of the major battles of the conflict were fought in whiskey-producing regions.

Prohibition wasn't much help, either, in keeping production going. Distilleries were closed and many never reopened. Six distilleries got licenses to produce whiskey for medicinal purposes, including Brown-Forman, which produces Woodford Reserve, and Stitzel-Weller, home to Julian "Pappy" Van Winkle Sr., who was an active distiller until age 89. After Prohibition the distillery produced Old Fitzgerald, Rebel Yell, and, since 1972, the Van Winkle labels.

In May 1964 the U.S. Congress declared bourbon to be "a distinctive product of the United States." It further went on to say that "the appropriate agencies of the United States Government are to take action to prohibit importation into the United States of whiskey designated as bourbon whiskey." There's more about this in the next section. And finally, in August 2007 the U.S. Senate passed a resolution declaring September 2007 "National Bourbon Heritage Month," marking the history of bourbon whiskey.

Some truth, some legend, and probably a little fiction cloud bourbon's history. Of course, that just makes it all the more fun!

WHAT ARE BOURBON AND ITS COUSIN, TENNESSEE WHISKEY?

When, knowing a good thing, Congress declared bourbon whiskey a "distinctive product of the United States" and "America's native spirit" back in 1964, it also established the Federal Standards of Identity for bourbon, which read in part:

- **Bourbon must be made of a grain mixture that is at least 51 percent corn. [The typical grain mixture used by distillers today is close to 70 to 75 percent corn.]**
- Bourbon must be distilled at no more than 160 proof, which is 80 percent alcohol by volume.
- **Bourbon must be 100 percent natural. Nothing other than water can be added.**
- **Bourbon must be aged in new, American, white oak barrels that have had their interiors charred by fire.**

Okay, once you have met all of the above requirements, then you have to age it. If it is aged for at least two years, the spirit can be labeled "straight bourbon," but there is no requirement to do so. In practice, today almost all bourbons are aged for at least four years. Bourbons aged for less than four years must label their aging duration. These are mostly inexpensive commodity brands.

Barrels can be used only once, thanks to the Federal Alcohol Administration Act passed in the mid-1930s. Arkansas Representative Wilbur Mills (yes, the guy of stripper-in-the-Tidal-Basin fame) was a major force in pushing this act through Congress. Most of the oak used in the distilling business came from Arkansas, so if you used a barrel only once, you had to buy more wood! After the barrels have done their magic in this country, they are sold to distillers in Scotland and Ireland. Seems that it takes a little bourbon leaching from the barrels to finish the taste profiles of many Scotch and Irish whiskies.

Notice not a word has been said about Tennessee whiskey. Neither I nor anyone else can find any legal U.S. definition, although there are international trade agreements that define Tennessee whiskey, and in 1941 Jack Daniel's Lem Motlow used the term to solicit a separate category from the government. Tennessee whiskey is essentially bourbon until it takes a 10-day drip through maple charcoal. This is called the Lincoln County Process, after the county where it was first practiced. The county lines have been redrawn so many times that the two distillers that use this process are no longer in Lincoln County. Some folks believe that this filtering smoothes out the spirit, making it more enjoyable, while others think the process removes way too much flavor and the essence of the spirit. I grew up on Jack Daniel's Old No. 7 Brand—it was my father's drink of choice. I have expanded my love of bourbon and Tennessee whiskey to include brands of both types. Each is distinct in its own way. The debate about bourbon versus Tennessee whiskey is much like the debate over who makes the best barbecue. The reality is that good producers make good products. The nuances are for you to discover and enjoy.

Mr. Jack, as in Daniel's, got his license to distill in 1866, and Jack Daniel's is the oldest licensed distillery. His Old No. 7 has plenty of legends surrounding its name, and it has become one of the largest-selling whiskies worldwide.

Here's a quick primer on how this golden, walnut-colored spirit is made. Most distillers use at least 70 percent corn, and 75 percent is not unheard of. The other grains included are wheat, rye (or a combination of both), and malted barley. The grain mixture, once some water is added, is known as the mash. Fermentation starts for most distillers by adding some of the yeast from the previous batch to the new one. This is called a "sour mash." You can start the process with a "sweet mash" using none of the previous batch's yeast, but a sour mash ensures consistent quality and flavor, the hallmarks of excellent master distillers.

The result of distilling is a clear spirit that's about 160 proof. Think perfect moonshine at this point. The liquid is then put into a charred oak barrel, from which it grabs color (longer aging means a darker color) as well as the beautiful vanilla and smoky caramel notes that make bourbon and Tennessee whiskey so distinctive and also mellow out the proof. After aging, the bourbon or Tennessee whiskey is diluted with the all-important water that has filtered through the limestone formations that predominate in western Kentucky and north-central Tennessee.

Most bourbons are diluted to around 80 proof, but 86 proof, 90 proof, and 100 proof are also common. There also proofs as high as 107 and up, such as Pappy Van Winkle's 15-year-old Family Reserve. Some bourbons are "barrel proof," and are labeled as such, meaning they have not been diluted and are bottled straight from the barrel. These are usually a much higher proof. Booker's, from the Jim Beam family, comes in at a "barrel" proof of 126.7, and George T. Stagg, from the Buffalo Trace folks, at an incredible 144.

SMALL-BATCH AND SINGLE-BARREL

Much of what is driving the increase in bourbon sales today is the phenomenon of small-batch and single-barrel varieties. *Small-batch* refers to bourbon that has been blended from selected barrels. This was part of the bourbon makers' response to the single-malt Scotch phenomenon that swept the country. Small-batch bourbons are typically aged for six to nine years in oak barrels, but there are more limited productions available that are aged up to 23 years, such as Pappy Van Winkle's Family Reserve. Other small-batch bourbons include Booker's, Woodford Reserve, and Basil Hayden. These bourbons are made for the true connoisseur and exhibit the artistry of these distillers' master distillers. Some have time-honored recipes dating back 200 years. In a recent tasting by cocktail.com, 15-year-old Rip Van Winkle ranked number one. The tasters seemed to like the caramel notes of this small-batch bourbon. A more widely distributed nine-year-old Knob Creek came in second.

Single-barrel bourbon or whiskey, as the name suggests, is a premium class of bourbon or Tennessee whiskey. Each bottle comes from an individual barrel with no blending from other barrels. This process creates unique differences from year to year. Much the way wine shifts its flavor profile through vintages, so does a single-barrel bourbon or Tennessee whiskey. Each bottle should carry the barrel number and, in most cases, the dates for the beginning and end of its aging. I find single-barrel bourbons a pleasant choice to sip slowly over a few cubes of ice. Try several to find the one you prefer, but remember, the next bottle will probably be different.

So now you know some interesting stuff about bourbon. Let's start pouring some.

STUFF YOU JUST NEED TO KNOW
GLASSWARE

Most of my early bourbon drinking experience involved a Solo cup. I never remember my dad using much more than a highball glass for his Jack Daniel's and 7UP. Point being, you don't need a lot of specialized glassware to drink bourbon. Remember that your first consideration is the quality of what you're putting in a glass. Any vessel will work for just about any drink. Rotgut bourbon and inferior fruit juice won't taste better just because you put them in a fancy glass. Spend your money first on ingredients, and then add glassware as you develop a repertoire of favorite drinks. All that said, though, here are some glasses I think you would enjoy having.

OLD-FASHIONED OR ROCKS GLASSES It was interesting to open a wedding present of these around teetotaling in-laws. My future mother-in-law said, "Aren't these beautiful juice glasses?" My future father-in-law said, "Those are old-fashioned glasses," since he had not always been a teetotaler. Old-fashioned glasses—or rocks glasses, as they are also called—usually hold 8 to 12 ounces and are typically short and round, but the more avant-garde can be square with rounded corners. Rocks glasses are used for drinks that are served over ice, or "on the rocks." I also like having what I call oversized old-fashioned glasses. Same shape, but taller, and usually hold 12 to 16 ounces. For many frozen drinks, these are perfect.

HIGHBALL GLASSES Highball glasses are basically just tall iced tea glasses. They are used mainly for drinks that contain some kind of soda or seltzer. Most highballs hold somewhere between 10 and 16 ounces of liquid. The tall, narrow shape keeps the bubbles intact longer than a shorter, wider glass would, allowing you to enjoy their effervescence longer. Close cousins of highball glasses are Collins glasses, which are taller and narrower.

COCKTAIL OR MARTINI GLASSES These stemmed, flared glasses are used for drinks served without ice—"straight up," in bar nomenclature. Of late, cocktail glasses fall all over the place in terms of size. They can be super-tiny, like 3 ounces, or oversized, coming in at about 10 ounces. Now think about that—almost 10 ounces of straight liquor? When I call for a cocktail glass, I'm referring to a standard, modern 6-ounce size.

CHAMPAGNE GLASSES Here I mean a champagne flute, which is the more elongated of the many styles of champagne glasses. It should hold 6 to 8 ounces and is wonderful for any drink that includes a sparkling wine.

BOURBON TASTING GLASSES Until recently, these were not part of the normal bar glassware display at your local store. Now they're easy to find at stores like Target and any good glassware shop. They are used to serve bourbon straight and unchilled. The bulb-shaped bottom aerates the bourbon, allowing the stronger vapors to dissipate. Although of course this book is all about cocktails, these are fun glasses to have if you and your buddies are doing a bourbon tasting or if you have some fine bourbons that you want to enjoy unadulterated.

PUNCH BOWL OR LARGE PITCHER These are great for parties. And if you anticipate doing a lot of those, I would invest in both. Cocktail pitchers seem to be the new generation's punch bowl. They tend to be tall and narrow, and usually come in sizes from 1 to 2 quarts. These are fine for mixing martinis for a small group, but try to find one that's 3 quarts or larger. Be sure that it has a pinched, rolled rim at the pouring end, which helps prevent the ice from coming out with the drink.

TOOLS THAT MAKE LIFE EASY

You can spend a fortune on bar equipment. But there are really only a few tools that you need, and those are the ones you should put your money into. You may already have a few in your kitchen.

JIGGERS Jiggers are nothing more than measuring cups. A lot of jiggers that you see on the market have long handles with two cups attached to one end. They measure 2 ounces on one side and 1 ounce on the other. I prefer the old shot-glass style that lists measurements from ¼ ounce to 2 ounces. And the really good ones show conversions of those ounce measurements into teaspoons, tablespoons, and milliliters. They are inexpensive and available most everywhere that sells glassware and bar equipment. Another item I've found that I like quite a bit is not really a jigger at all, but a ¼-cup measuring cup made by OXO. It has a pinched pouring spout, which keeps things a little neater. You can also pick up from a restaurant supply store bottle toppers that accurately measure out 1, 1½, or 2 ounces. You've probably seen these in some bars; many states require them so that you don't get "short pours."

SHAKERS There are two types of cocktail shakers. One is known in the trade as a "cobbler" shaker. This shaker, which comes in multiple sizes, is usually stainless steel and has a snug-fitting top with a built-in strainer. There's also a smaller cap that covers the strainer and in many cases can double as a jigger. Put the ice and the cocktail ingredients in the base, put on the top and the cap, and shake vigorously until the metal begins to frost. Then remove the cap, and strain into a glass.

The other type of shaker, which is the one that you see bartenders use most frequently, is a Boston shaker. It consists of two parts, a metal body that usually holds around 24 ounces and a glass that holds about 16 ounces. You fill the glass

Bardstown, Kentucky, is the declared "Bourbon Capital of the World," and during the third weekend of September the city hosts the Kentucky Bourbon Festival. For more information, check kybourbonfestival.com.

with ice and the cocktail ingredients, then you put the metal body over the glass and gently tap until the two seal. Press the metal shaker into your palm and put a couple of fingers on top of the glass shaker. Shake, leaving the liquid and ice in the metal shaker when done. To break the seal, tap the metal shaker with the heel of your hand. You will need some sort of strainer for pouring (see below). This all looks really good if you're a high-end bartender in one of the many top drinking establishments across the country. I find Boston shakers to be generally a pain in the rear.

STRAINERS That funky-looking strainer with a metal coil around its underside is known as the "Hawthorn" strainer. If you have a Boston shaker, a Hawthorn strainer, which is used over the shaker bottom, is absolutely necessary. The other type of strainer is what's known as a julep, which looks a bit like an old-style tea strainer, with little holes perforating the metal surface. It's used over the serving glass. The Hawthorn strainer is used almost exclusively for shaken drinks and the julep for stirred drinks.

COCKTAIL SPOONS These long-handled spoons are used to stir drinks in individual glasses or in pitchers. The twisted handle design makes it easy to rotate the spoon through the drink. A long-handled iced tea spoon works almost as well. When stirring drinks, make sure condensation develops on the outside of the container, an indication that the drink is cold enough; this takes 15 to 20 seconds. By the way, don't stir like you would paddle a boat against the current in the Mississippi River. Slow is better.

MUDDLERS If you're going to make mint juleps, you're going to need a muddler. It is used to mash fruit and herbs, usually with the help of a little sugar to act as an abrasive. It looks like a 6-inch-long miniature baseball bat with one flat end. Unvarnished wood is the best type to buy, and they are inexpensive. However, while working on this book I was introduced to a plastic muddler at the Greenbrier hotel and resort in West Virginia. I have since purchased one and use it almost exclusively.

JUICERS If you're going to use good bourbon, you really need to give it the freshest ingredients, and that especially includes fruit juices. You will need a citrus juicer or reamer. There are many types available, like the handheld wooden ones that you push into the fruit, the ones that look like oversized garlic presses (which are fun, but you need three for the different sizes of citrus fruit), or some version of that old-style glass juicer with the ridged knob in the middle. Anything that lets you squeeze out fresh juice is a beautiful thing.

KNIVES, ZESTERS, AND GRATERS It may sound a little condescending for me to tell you that you need a knife. A good 3- or 4-inch paring knife is perfect for slicing lemons and such, but you probably also will need an 8-inch chef's knife for cutting larger fruit, such as pineapple. A channel knife is that funny-looking thing with a round head and a small curved blade that seems to pop out from the hole in the center of the head. Use this for cutting long citrus peel swirls. Many channel knives are dual-purpose, with a zester on top of the head or at the other end of the handle. You can also buy a zester as an individual tool, which I think is better because typically they are sturdier and cut better. You should also have some sort of small grater. There are volumes of difference in taste between pre-ground and freshly grated nutmeg. Having a little nutmeg grater is a nice thing, but the Microplane graters work just as well and have multiple uses.

"SHAKEN, NOT STIRRED"... USING THE RIGHT TECHNIQUE

Now let's look at a few basic methods. Again, I'm thinking about the home bartender and how to convert the professional methods to personal ones. To shake or stir—the James Bond question. The only real rule of thumb that seems to be consistent among bartenders is that shaking a drink is preferred when drinks contain juices, an egg or egg white, creamy ingredients, or other relatively high-viscosity ingredients. To know when you've shaken a drink enough, look for the shaker to be frosted and beaded with condensation. This process takes 15 to 20 seconds. But shaking a drink is not a salsa dance; it's more like a waltz. You need consistent rhythm to ensure the drink is mixed efficiently.

Stirring, most bartenders believe, is for drinks that contain mostly liquor, a martini being a perfect example. Bartenders around the country have told me that stirring liquor produces a more delicate texture. I had never thought about texture in a martini, but when I had a bartender fix me two martinis, one shaken and one stirred, there was a slightly noticeable difference between the two. It's your house, so experiment and make up your own rules.

MUDDLING Most of us think of muddling with mint juleps. But any herb or fruit can be muddled with a little sugar in the bottom of a large glass or your cocktail shaker. To muddle, use the flat end of the muddler, press down firmly on the fruit or herb, and then twist the tool, breaking down the fruit or herb to release as much essential oil and juice as possible. Keep rotating around the glass until everything resembles a soft puree or the herbs are sufficiently torn up.

TASTY ADDITIONS

Let me just breeze through a few ingredients that you need to have on hand for cocktail making.

PEYCHAUD'S BITTERS Antoine Amédée Peychaud of New Orleans first produced his bitters in the early 1800s. The pharmacists used bitters as a cure-all for everything. (And a little bitters in soda is still a good way to calm the stomach. But Peychaud's claim that his bitters would cure anything that caused your misery was a bit off.) These bitters are slightly cherry or black currant in flavor. They are a great balance to sweeter cocktails and where I've included them in this book's recipes, you should use them.

ANGOSTURA BITTERS These bitters were first produced in Venezuela in their namesake town by a Dr. J. G. B. Siegert in 1824 and first exported to London in 1830. They are the most widely known and used of the bitters family. They're dark, strong in flavor, very herbaceous, and a little sweet. Up until recently, unless you were in or around New Orleans, if a drink called for bitters, this is what you got. But as mixologists have honed their craft, they've found that different takes on bitters can have a great impact on a cocktail. And by the way, there's no longer a town by the name of Angostura in Venezuela. It's now called Ciudad Bolívar.

FLAVORED BITTERS Orange bitters are the most widely used flavored bitters today. When a bit of orange essence is desired, reach for these bitters. Lemon, lime, and peach bitters can also be useful. Fee Brothers is a good label, and other artisanal bitters companies are springing up all over.

Check out kentuckybourbontrail.com for an interesting ride through bourbon country. For a wider view, visit americanwhiskeytrail.com. Here you will find a comprehensive view of the distilling history of the United States.

HOT SAUCE Hot sauce and bourbon? Before you even ask, don't knock it until you've tried it. Anytime you want to intensify the heat of a cocktail, use a hot sauce. Every brand of hot sauce has its own nuance, and much like your favorite style of barbecue, pick the one you like. My favorite brands are Texas Pete, Crystal, Frank's, and Tabasco original and chipotle. You might want to keep two or three on hand just for variation.

SUGAR No matter what the recipe, you can always use plain old regular granulated sugar. But many times superfine sugar or confectioners' sugar is preferable. Superfine, or what some people refer to as bar sugar, may not be sitting on your grocer's shelf. If you can't find it, throw some regular sugar into a food processor and process until fine. And not that I'm saying you would, but just in case, don't try rimming a glass with confectioners' sugar. It has cornstarch in it and just doesn't work very well for that purpose.

ICE Ice has an effect on the final flavor of cocktails. Using filtered water to make it is always best, and it's simple with the refrigerators that have built-in filtered water dispensers, or with the many pitchers and other devices that can filter tap water. You don't want any chemicals to detract from that good limestone water used in distilling those bourbons and Tennessee whiskies. Ice also affects the drink's strength as it melts. In Japan a good bar will actually craft a "rock" when you order whiskey on the rocks. It is a single ball of ice meant to keep the melting rate slow. Tailor in New York City uses square blocks of ice for the same purpose. Some drinks get shards of ice to control the melting rate in a different way. Now, I'm not suggesting that you do the same, but at least think about your ice. A mint julep demands crushed ice, which, by melting more rapidly, becomes part of the cocktail. Cubes should be used when less melting is desired. I've indicated the type of ice for most of the cocktails, so please follow the suggestions. Ice may seem like a small detail, yet it has a big impact.

SIMPLE SYRUP FROM SCRATCH

MAKES 1 CUP

Simple syrup is a bartender's friend. It makes sweetening drinks easy, eliminates any grittiness, and also can be used to sweeten iced tea, lemonade, and such. It will keep for at least a couple of weeks in your refrigerator in a covered container.

1 CUP SUGAR
1 CUP WATER

Stir together the sugar and water in a small saucepan. Place over medium heat and slowly bring to a boil, stirring until the sugar dissolves and the liquid is slightly syrupy. Remove from the heat and let the syrup cool before using.

NOTE: Simple syrup can be made in any amount depending on how fast you intend to use it. I always make it from equal parts sugar and water. I like to store my simple syrup in a squeeze bottle, which gives me quick access and a non-messy way to sweeten drinks.

For Vanilla Simple Syrup, a great variation, split 1 vanilla bean and add the seeds and pod to the saucepan along with the sugar and water. Proceed as directed, simmering for about 2 minutes and removing the pod after the syrup cools (you don't have to remove the seeds). At my house, most of the time I use Vanilla Simple Syrup. It gives your taste buds an "Mmm . . . That's really good and slightly different, but it's really good" kind of effect.

HOMEMADE SOUR MIX

MAKES 6 CUPS

Sour mix is probably one of the most versatile flavoring devices at the bar, and recipes in this book make use of it. There is no comparison between homemade sour mix and the store-bought stuff. None. Zippo. Making sour mix is easy, and it will impress the daylights out of anyone you make a drink for. Not to mention what it will do for your own personal enjoyment. Some sour mix recipes call for either all lemons or all limes. I like the juxtaposition of the two. This keeps in the refrigerator for 2 weeks or frozen for 1 month.

> 2 CUPS FRESHLY SQUEEZED AND STRAINED LEMON JUICE
> (FROM 12 TO 14 LEMONS)
> 2 CUPS FRESHLY SQUEEZED AND STRAINED LIME JUICE
> (FROM 12 TO 14 LIMES)
> 1 CUP PASTEURIZED EGG WHITES (SEE NOTE)
> 1 CUP SIMPLE SYRUP (OPPOSITE PAGE)

Combine both juices in a bowl. Mix in the egg whites and simple syrup and whisk thoroughly. Strain this mixture into a container with a lid. You should taste the mix to check on its tart/sweet relationship and adjust as desired by adding extra citrus juice or more simple syrup. Cover and chill before using.

> **NOTE:** Look for pasteurized egg whites at your local grocery store. Some come in clear plastic containers in the refrigerated case, with no color added. There are also a couple of brands of just egg whites in pint milk-type cartons. Just be sure to read the ingredients and make sure no color has been added. Egg Beaters and the like are not what you want for making this mix.

THE CLASSICS

The word *classic* gets thrown around with great ease in today's world. By my daughter's measure, I'm a classic, meaning I've been around for a long time. My definition of a classic is something that has stood the test of time, developed a sense of history and place, established a tradition, and most of all, set a standard for things to come. The classics of the cocktail world have earned their right to be in this category. Over time, also, many classics have been tinkered with, and those variations have become so accepted that they have become "new classics." You'll find some of those here as well.

When we look at classic cocktails containing bourbon, we find a wealth of drinks. From the Manhattan Club in New York City to the Pendennis Club in Louisville, from the Greenbrier Hotel in West Virginia to Pat O'Brien's in New Orleans, serious students of the craft of bartending have given us great examples and awesome flavors. Manhattans, Old Fashioneds, Mint Juleps, Whiskey Sours—they are all still relevant today because of skilled bartenders. These cocktails are to be savored, sipped slowly to allow all the nuances of the bourbon to develop and mingle with its complements in the glass. From that delightful experience comes pleasure, and meditation, the epitome of a spirit. Of course, the greatest classic of bourbon "cocktails" is just bourbon on the rocks, followed closely by "bourbon and branch," a simple concoction of three parts bourbon to one part spring water. These classics have become the foundation for the cocktails that follow. Take some time with them and stroll through the ages.

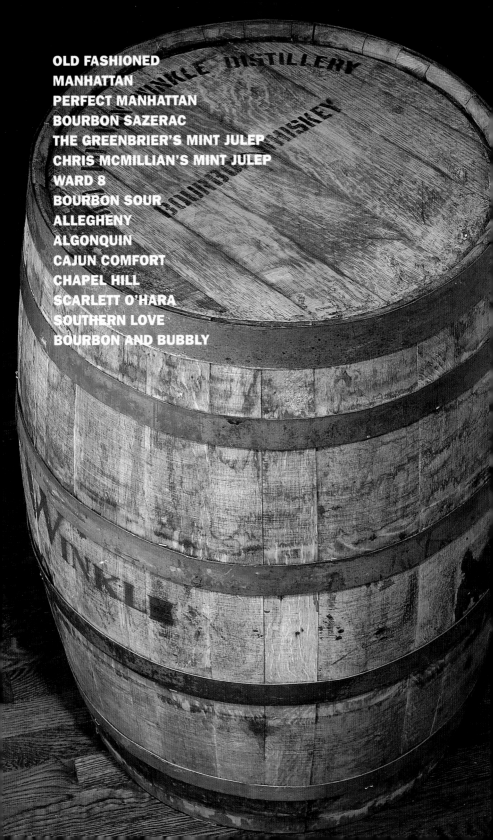

OLD FASHIONED
MANHATTAN
PERFECT MANHATTAN
BOURBON SAZERAC
THE GREENBRIER'S MINT JULEP
CHRIS MCMILLIAN'S MINT JULEP
WARD 8
BOURBON SOUR
ALLEGHENY
ALGONQUIN
CAJUN COMFORT
CHAPEL HILL
SCARLETT O'HARA
SOUTHERN LOVE
BOURBON AND BUBBLY

OLD FASHIONED

SERVES 1

The Pendennis Club in Louisville, Kentucky, lays claim to being the birthplace of the Old Fashioned. It was first mixed either by or in honor of Colonel James E. Pepper, a proprietor of a celebrated whiskey distillery of the period. The first record of the Old Fashioned in print is in *Modern American Drinks* (1895) by George J. Kappeler.

2 DASHES PEYCHAUD'S BITTERS

1 TEASPOON SIMPLE SYRUP (PAGE 18), OR TO TASTE

1 MARASCHINO CHERRY

1 ORANGE SLICE

2 OUNCES BOURBON

ICE CUBES

1 Combine the bitters, simple syrup, cherry, and orange in an old-fashioned glass. Muddle until a paste forms.

2 Pour in the bourbon, fill with ice cubes, and stir until well combined. Serve immediately.

MANHATTAN

SERVES 2

The Manhattan Club. It sounds like a serious place for power brokers in New York City in the late 1800s. Serious money and serious power yield a serious drink, one of great sophistication and one that allows a certain amount of variation. Bourbon, with its hint of smokiness and generally a bit more bite than other brown liquors, became the alcohol of choice for most classic Manhattan drinkers over rye whiskey, which was at one time the standard. Drink this cocktail with panache.

ICE CUBES
4½ OUNCES BOURBON
1½ OUNCES SWEET VERMOUTH
2 DASHES ANGOSTURA BITTERS
DASH OF MARASCHINO CHERRY JUICE
2 MARASCHINO CHERRIES

1 Fill a large cocktail shaker halfway full with ice cubes. Add the bourbon, sweet vermouth, bitters, and cherry juice. Shake vigorously until the drink is extremely cold.

2 Place a cherry in each of two cocktail glasses, and strain the drink equally between the glasses. Serve immediately.

VARIATION: A dry Manhattan is a wonderful apéritif. Simply substitute dry vermouth or Lillet Blanc for the sweet vermouth. Replace the cherries with lemon twists and proceed as above.

PERFECT MANHATTAN

SERVES 2

The Perfect is a more current take on the Manhattan, but it still qualifies as a classic. What makes it "perfect" is the use of both sweet and dry vermouth, which creates a unique Manhattan that is both dry and slightly sweet at the same time. Very refreshing.

ICE CUBES
4½ OUNCES BOURBON
¾ OUNCE DRY VERMOUTH
¾ OUNCE SWEET VERMOUTH
2 DASHES ANGOSTURA BITTERS
2 LEMON TWISTS

1 Fill a large cocktail shaker halfway full with ice cubes. Add the bourbon, both vermouths, and the bitters. Shake until the drink is extremely cold.

2 Strain the drink into two cocktail glasses. Twist a lemon twist over each drink to release the oils, and then drop it in. Serve immediately.

BOURBON SAZERAC

SERVES 4

This New Orleans creation, originally developed by Antoine Peychaud, a local apothecary, was made with brandy, absinthe, and a dash of Peychaud's secret blend of bitters. Its popularity became apparent when it was served at the Sazerac Coffee House, where it was made only with a local brandy called Sazerac de Forge et Fils. Soon, rye whiskey became more favored than brandy for making this drink. Some of the ritual of how Sazeracs were made during the days before absinthe was banned is gone (though the absinthe ban has been lifted). A bourbon Sazerac will give the feel of the French Quarter.

CRACKED ICE
2 TEASPOONS PERNOD
ICE CUBES
8 OUNCES BOURBON
2½ OUNCES SIMPLE SYRUP (PAGE 18)
20 DASHES PEYCHAUD'S BITTERS
4 LEMON TWISTS

1 Place a few pieces of cracked ice in each of 4 cocktail glasses. Add ½ teaspoon Pernod to each glass. Stir, and then set aside.

2 Fill a pitcher or large cocktail shaker halfway full with ice cubes. Add the bourbon, simple syrup, and bitters. Stir or shake until the drink is extremely cold.

3 Pour out the ice and the liquid from the cocktail glasses. Add some fresh cracked ice to each, and strain the drink equally into the glasses. Twist a lemon twist over each glass to release the oils, drop it in, and serve.

THE GREENBRIER'S MINT JULEP

SERVES 2

The mint julep's history is about as muddled as the mint in this drink. Some say it was the Virginians who first took this drink, while others believe it originated in Kentucky. Rather than using simple syrup, as most do now, it originally called for sugar and water to be muddled with the mint. The Greenbrier hotel and resort was probably the first to offer the julep, at its lobby bar, and more than likely gussied it up with a silver cup. This is very close to that recipe. What might surprise you is that this was originally a morning pick-me-up beverage for farmers and stable hands. What a great alternative to coffee! The crushed ice is essential for the enjoyment of this drink.

12 FRESH MINT SPRIGS, PLUS 2 SPRIGS FOR GARNISH
2 OUNCES SIMPLE SYRUP (PAGE 18)
CRUSHED ICE
4 OUNCES BOURBON (PREFERABLY MAKER'S MARK)

1 Place 2 old-fashioned glasses or julep cups in the freezer for about 15 minutes.

2 Place 6 mint sprigs and 1 ounce simple syrup in the bottom of each glass. Muddle until the mint is crushed.

3 Fill the glasses with crushed ice and divide the bourbon between the glasses. Stir until the glasses are frosted and the drink is extremely cold. Garnish with the remaining mint, and serve.

CHRIS McMILLIAN'S MINT JULEP

SERVES 1

At the Bar on Common in New Orleans's Renaissance Pere Marquette Hotel, Chris McMillian reigns supreme. His thoughts on the mint julep? "Who has not tasted one has lived in vain," he says. "It is the very dream of drinks, the vision of sweet quaffings." He is an original. "Chris is a rare living link to this amazing old-world profession," says Dave Wondrich, drinks correspondent for *Esquire* and author of *Imbibe!* (Perigee Books, 2007). "There are plenty of creative younger bartenders who know how to mix, but very few who have mastered the lore and demeanor of the old days." Chris's mint juleps may not be traditional, but they are damn good. As he serves you, he recites from the ode to the mint julep written in the 1890s by a Kentucky newspaperman. The last stanza really sums up the drink and this entire book. "Sip it and dream— it is a dream itself," it goes. "Sip it and say there is no solace for the soul, no tonic for the body like old Bourbon whiskey."

12 TO 15 FRESH MINT LEAVES, PLUS 1 SPRIG FOR GARNISH
1 OUNCE PEACH SYRUP, SUCH AS MONIN
FINELY CRUSHED ICE
2½ OUNCES BOURBON
SUPERFINE SUGAR

1 Place the mint and ¼ ounce of the peach syrup in a julep cup or old-fashioned glass and gently crush the mint leaves with a wooden muddler, working them up the sides of the glass.

2 Loosely pack the glass with finely crushed ice, then add your bourbon. Drizzle the remaining peach syrup on top. Lightly dust the mint sprig with sugar, and garnish the drink with it. Serve immediately.

WARD 8

SERVES 2

Legend has it that this drink was created in Boston in the late 1800s to either celebrate or bemoan the city being districted into eight wards. I think you will enjoy this blending of smoky bourbon and orange.

ICE CUBES
4 OUNCES BOURBON
2 OUNCES SIMPLE SYRUP (PAGE 18)
2 OUNCES FRESHLY SQUEEZED ORANGE JUICE (FROM ABOUT ½ ORANGE)
1½ OUNCES FRESHLY SQUEEZED LEMON JUICE (FROM ABOUT 1 LEMON)
½ OUNCE GRENADINE
2 ORANGE SLICES, FOR GARNISH
2 MARASCHINO CHERRIES, FOR GARNISH

1 Fill a cocktail shaker halfway full with ice cubes and add the bourbon, simple syrup, orange juice, lemon juice, and grenadine. Shake vigorously until the shaker is frosty.

2 Fill 2 old-fashioned glasses with ice cubes. Strain the mixture equally into each glass. Garnish each with an orange slice and a cherry, and serve.

BOURBON SOUR

This cocktail is the yin and yang of bourbon flavors. Sweet, tangy, and a bit bold—it is one of the most ordered cocktails in bars everywhere. It is an extremely refreshing drink when made with fresh juice versus a powdered mix.

ICE CUBES

12 OUNCES BOURBON

5 OUNCES FRESHLY SQUEEZED LEMON JUICE (FROM ABOUT 4 LEMONS)

1 OUNCE SIMPLE SYRUP (PAGE 18)

6 MARASCHINO CHERRIES, FOR GARNISH

1 Fill a cocktail shaker halfway full with ice cubes. Add the bourbon, lemon juice, and simple syrup. Shake briskly until the shaker is frosted.

2 Strain the cocktail equally into 6 old-fashioned or cocktail glasses, garnish each with a cherry, and serve.

> NOTE: If you like, substitute the homemade sour mix on page 19 for the lemon juice and the simple syrup. Start with about 5 ounces of the sour mix and adjust to your liking.

ALLEGHENY

SERVES 1

This is an old-style cocktail that probably had its beginnings as a variation of the Manhattan. The blackberry brandy lets this concoction just scream *Southern*.

ICE CUBES
1 OUNCE DRY VERMOUTH
1 OUNCE BOURBON
1 TEASPOON BLACKBERRY BRANDY
1 TEASPOON FRESHLY SQUEEZED LEMON JUICE
1 LEMON TWIST, FOR GARNISH

1 Fill a cocktail shaker halfway full with ice cubes. Add the vermouth, bourbon, brandy, and lemon juice. Shake vigorously until the shaker is frosted.

2 Strain into a cocktail glass, and garnish with the lemon twist. Serve immediately.

ALGONQUIN

SERVES 1

Did Dorothy Parker ever have one of these? I don't know. But she certainly drank a lot at the Algonquin Bar, as have the other primary players for *The New Yorker* magazine. This is one of their special cocktails that has been around for years.

ICE CUBES
2 OUNCES BOURBON
1 OUNCE DRY VERMOUTH
1 OUNCE FRESH PINEAPPLE JUICE
1 MARASCHINO CHERRY, FOR GARNISH

1 Fill a cocktail shaker halfway full with ice cubes. Pour in the bourbon, vermouth, and pineapple juice. Using a bar spoon or iced tea spoon, gently stir until the drink is very cold.

2 Pour the entire mixture into an old-fashioned glass, or strain the mixture into a cocktail glass. Garnish with the cherry, and serve immediately.

CAJUN COMFORT

SERVES 1

Even when it comes to beverages, Cajuns like things spicy. You could heat up this drink even more by using a habanero hot sauce.

ICE CUBES
1½ OUNCES BOURBON
1 OUNCE SOUTHERN COMFORT
2 TABLESPOONS HONEY
4 OR 5 DASHES HOT SAUCE

1 Fill a cocktail shaker halfway full with ice cubes. Add the bourbon, Southern Comfort, honey, and hot sauce. Shake slowly, allowing the honey to incorporate, until the shaker is frosted.

2 Pour the mixture, ice and all, into an old-fashioned glass. Serve immediately.

CHAPEL HILL

SERVES 1

A graduation drink for the University of North Carolina at Chapel Hill, this one's too good to reserve just for celebrations.

ICE CUBES
1½ OUNCES BOURBON
½ OUNCE TRIPLE SEC
½ OUNCE FRESHLY SQUEEZED LEMON JUICE
1 ORANGE TWIST, FOR GARNISH

1 Fill a cocktail shaker halfway full with ice cubes. Pour the bourbon, triple sec, and lemon juice into the shaker, and shake until the drink is cold.

2 Strain into a cocktail glass. Garnish with the orange twist, and serve.

SCARLETT O'HARA

SERVES 2

Shortly after *Gone with the Wind* became the hit and then classic motion picture that it is, this recipe was developed to pay tribute to the heroine of the movie. It's made with Southern Comfort, which is a sweetened, fruit-infused bourbon. Southern Comfort has sometimes been the butt of jokes, but on a hot afternoon, some on the rocks is pretty doggone good.

ICE CUBES
4 OUNCES SOUTHERN COMFORT
2 OUNCES FRESHLY SQUEEZED LIME JUICE (FROM ABOUT 2 LIMES)
4 OUNCES CRANBERRY JUICE
2 LIME WEDGES, FOR GARNISH

1 Fill a cocktail shaker halfway full with ice cubes. Add the Southern Comfort, lime juice, and cranberry juice. Shake briskly until the shaker is frosty.

2 Strain into 2 cocktail glasses, garnish each with a lime wedge, and serve.

> **VARIATION:** We certainly can't forget Rhett Butler with all this drink creation, but I bet he would have liked a cocktail with a little more kick: Make the Scarlett O'Hara as directed, but add 2 ounces Grand Marnier to the other liquids. Rhett didn't give a damn, but I imagine that extra shot of orange-flavored liqueur would make him enjoy this somewhat fruity concoction.

SOUTHERN LOVE
SERVES 1

For all you lovers of bourbon and cola, here's an upgraded, fancy-pants rendition that you serve in a cocktail glass. Even if you're not a bourbon and cola fan, you might change your mind after a sip or two of this drink. I know I did.

ICE CUBES
1 OUNCE BOURBON
1 OUNCE AMARETTO
6 OUNCES COLA

1 Fill an oversized cocktail or old-fashioned glass with ice cubes. Let it sit for 2 or 3 minutes to chill the glass.

2 Holding the ice so it doesn't fall out, discard any melted water. Pour in the bourbon and amaretto, and top with the cola. Stir and serve immediately.

BOURBON AND BUBBLY

SERVES 8

Bourbon with the effervescent touch of sparkling wine is a combination that tickles your mouth as you drink it and can tickle your brain later on. This is a takeoff on the signature cocktail from Louisville's famed Seelbach Hilton, and it's wonderful to serve to a crowd. Try this as an apéritif before your Thanksgiving meal. I can almost guarantee no familial fighting.

4 OUNCES BOURBON
4 TABLESPOONS SUGAR
1 TEASPOON ANGOSTURA BITTERS
ICE CUBES
EIGHT 2-INCH STRIPS LEMON PEEL (NO PITH)
ONE 750-MILLILITER BOTTLE VERY COLD, VERY DRY CHAMPAGNE OR
    SPARKLING WINE

1 Mix the bourbon, sugar, and bitters in a glass measuring cup. Let stand until the sugar begins to dissolve, stirring occasionally. This will take 10 to 15 minutes (you can make this 4 or more hours ahead, if you wish).

2 Add ice cubes to 8 small wine glasses. Twist a piece of lemon peel over each glass, and drop in. Divide the bourbon mixture among the wine glasses, and then fill the glasses with Champagne. Serve immediately.

UPDATED, NEWFANGLED, AND FULL OF FRUIT

Remember that the classic cocktails serve as standard-bearers of things to come and invite innovation. As you journey through this wide-open chapter, notice those cocktails that have most been influenced by tradition. Also consider what you might glean from this chapter to spark your own personality and creativity. Cocktail making is a fluid state (no pun intended), always changing with new ideas and as new products become available.

These recipes will surprise you by their width and depth. You may find blends that you would have never thought of with bourbon, such as the wide range of fruit that marries so well with the typical vanilla and caramel tones of bourbon. I certainly hadn't considered bourbon and basil or blueberries until I slurped oysters and had a lesson on mixology at the Bourbon House in New Orleans. The thought of cardamom and bourbon seemed so out of place until I tried it, with honey and Van Winkle bourbon, at Eleven Madison Park in New York City.

We are certainly in the middle of a rebirth and renaissance of cocktails, and a new appreciation for bourbon. Imbibe with gusto and dive into the new wave.

NEW FASHIONED
BLUEGRASS SUNSET
STREET CAR
SLAP AND TICKLE
WASHINGTON APPLE
LYNCHBURG LEMONADE
ELEVEN MADISON PARK'S HONEY AND CARDAMOM
  BOURBON
THE BROOKLYN, OR NOT QUITE A MANHATTAN
THE BOURBON "ORANGE THING"
BOURBON RUSSIAN
MANGO BOURBON SLING
BOURBON BOG
UMBRIAN MANHATTAN
COMMANDER'S PALACE INCREDIBLE MILK PUNCH
NATCHEZ BELLE

NEW FASHIONED

SERVES 1

This recipe came out of a trip that Dickie Brennan and key members of his Bourbon House restaurant in New Orleans made to Kentucky. There was a lot of discussion about updating classic bourbon cocktails, and one thought included the produce bounty of Louisiana and the Gulf Coast. The New Fashioned incorporates seasonal fruit. You can use peaches, strawberries, blueberries, or even raspberries to concoct this sinfully good cocktail.

¼ CUP MACERATED PEACHES (SEE NOTE)
5 DASHES PEYCHAUD'S BITTERS
SPLASH OF SIMPLE SYRUP (PAGE 18)
SPLASH OF CLUB SODA
2 OUNCES HIGH-QUALITY BOURBON (PREFERABLY KNOB CREEK)
ICE CUBES

1 Place the macerated peaches, bitters, simple syrup, and soda in an old-fashioned glass and muddle.

2 Add the bourbon, fill with ice cubes, and stir until well mixed. Serve immediately.

NOTE: "Macerating" seems to be a highfalutin word for something that is extremely simple. All you do is sprinkle chopped fruit with a bit of sugar and refrigerate overnight. The sugar draws out the juices, and your fruit basically marinates in its own juice.

BLUEGRASS SUNSET

SERVES 1

One of the bartenders for the Brennan family in New Orleans needed to create a drink that could illustrate "muddling" for a cocktails event. He decided to incorporate ingredients that were in season and local—basil and satsuma oranges. The name of the drink was bestowed to honor the beautiful bourbon state of Kentucky.

> SPLASH OF SIMPLE SYRUP (PAGE 18)
> 1 FRESH BASIL SPRIG
> 1 SLICE SATSUMA OR NAVEL ORANGE
> CRUSHED ICE
> 1½ OUNCES BOURBON (PREFERABLY KENTUCKY SPIRIT)
> SPLASH OF GINGER ALE
> SPLASH OF SODA WATER

1 Put a splash of simple syrup in the bottom of an old-fashioned glass. Add the basil sprig and orange slice and muddle until the basil and orange have released their aromas.

2 Fill the glass to the top with crushed ice. Add the bourbon and top with a splash each of ginger ale and soda. Serve immediately.

NOTE: What the heck is a satsuma? It's nothing more than a seedless mandarin orange, and it has quite a bit of oil encased in its rind.

STREET CAR

SERVES 1

Sitting around the oyster bar at the Bourbon House in New Orleans with my friends from The Harvard Common Press, we were slurping down oysters before a bourbon–food pairing event that we were going to attend upstairs. Up on the wall above the bar was a mention of a "street car" as a bourbon-based drink. So I inquired. It seems it was developed by Christy Campbell, a member of the Bourbon House family. During blueberry season she wanted to incorporate them in a cocktail that had a link to New Orleans. The result is very close to a classic Sidecar. And while I snickered at this idea to begin with, once tasted, everyone agreed that it was a wonderful and delicious cocktail and that we needed to include it in this book.

ICE CUBES
2 OUNCES BOURBON (PREFERABLY ELMER T. LEE)
½ OUNCE CRÈME DE CASSIS
SPLASH OF VANILLA SIMPLE SYRUP (PAGE 18)
JUICE OF 1 LIME
1 TABLESPOON BLUEBERRY COMPOTE (I OFTEN USE HIGH-QUALITY
   PRESERVES INSTEAD OF MAKING COMPOTE)
FRESH BLUEBERRIES FOR GARNISH

1 Fill a cocktail shaker halfway full with ice cubes. Combine the bourbon, crème de cassis, vanilla simple syrup, lime juice, and blueberry compote in the shaker. Shake vigorously until the drink is well chilled.

2 Strain into a cocktail glass. Garnish with a few blueberries, and serve immediately.

SLAP AND TICKLE

SERVES 1

Why such an absurd name? Because it's exactly what this beverage will do to you if you overindulge. Think of this as a Deep South–Long Island iced tea. It goes down very smoothly but with quite a punch.

ICE CUBES
1 OUNCE BOURBON
1 OUNCE BRANDY
½ OUNCE SOUTHERN COMFORT
1 OUNCE VODKA
1 OUNCE RUBY RED GRAPEFRUIT JUICE
3 OUNCES FRESH PINEAPPLE JUICE
1 OUNCE FRESHLY SQUEEZED ORANGE JUICE (FROM ABOUT ¼ ORANGE)
1 TABLESPOON GRENADINE

1 Fill a cocktail shaker halfway full with ice cubes. Add the bourbon, brandy, Southern Comfort, vodka, all the juices, and the grenadine to the shaker. Shake vigorously until the drink is cold.

2 Fill a highball glass halfway full with ice cubes, and strain the concoction into the glass. Serve immediately.

WASHINGTON APPLE

SERVES 1

At a barbecue festival in Franklin, Tennessee, I ran into a young woman named Amanda, who told me about this recipe. It's absolutely delicious and seems to be trendy throughout the country. Think of it as a Cosmopolitan with brown liquor.

ICE CUBES
1½ OUNCES BOURBON
1½ OUNCES APPLE PUCKER
1½ OUNCES CRANBERRY JUICE
1 APPLE SLICE OR WEDGE (EVEN BETTER IS A DRIED APPLE SLICE),
  FOR GARNISH

1 Fill a cocktail shaker halfway full with ice cubes. Pour the bourbon, Pucker, and cranberry juice into the shaker. Shake vigorously until the drink is cold.

2 Strain into a cocktail glass. Garnish with the apple, and serve.

LYNCHBURG LEMONADE
SERVES 1

This is a wonderful summertime back-porch rocking-chair kind of cocktail. It's named after Lynchburg, Tennessee, the home of Jack Daniel's distillery, where you can't order this anywhere because unfortunately Lynchburg is "dry." There are a hundred variations of Lynchburg Lemonade—this just happens to be my favorite. Tinker with it if you desire to make it your perfect rocking-chair cocktail. This almost ranks as a classic.

ICE CUBES
1½ OUNCES JACK DANIEL'S OR OTHER TENNESSEE WHISKEY
1 OUNCE TRIPLE SEC
1 OUNCE SOUR MIX (PAGE 19)
LEMON-LIME SODA AS NEEDED

Fill a highball glass with ice cubes. Add the Jack Daniel's, triple sec, and sour mix, and stir to combine. Top off the glass with the lemon-lime soda and head for the porch.

ELEVEN MADISON PARK'S HONEY AND CARDAMOM BOURBON

SERVES 6

For the last several years one of New York's top restaurateurs, Danny Meyer, has brought the joy of barbecue and music to Madison Square Park. The Big Apple Barbecue Block Party is an event that every Manhattanite with no grill looks forward to. One of Danny's restaurants across from the park teams up with the Van Winkle distillery and serves mint juleps and creates a special bourbon drink each year. This is one that I thought was particularly good. A little flavor of mystery dancing with the bourbon. If you don't use all the cardamom-infused honey, it keeps covered in the refrigerator for several weeks.

> **FOR THE INFUSED HONEY:**
> ½ CUP HONEY
> 1½ CUPS BOILING WATER
> 10 TO 12 CARDAMOM SEEDS (FROM 1 POD)
> **FOR THE DRINK:**
> ICE CUBES
> 12 OUNCES HIGH-QUALITY BOURBON (SINGLE-BARREL PREFERRED)
> 6 LEMON TWISTS
> CLUB SODA AS NEEDED (OPTIONAL)

1 To make the infused honey, stir together the honey and boiling water in a heatproof measuring cup. Add the cardamom seeds, cover, and let steep for 2 to 4 hours.

2 To make the drink, fill 6 old-fashioned glasses with ice cubes. Add 2 ounces of bourbon to each glass along with 3 ounces of the infused honey. Twist a lemon twist over each drink, then drop it in. Stir and serve. If desired, add a splash of club soda to soften the drink.

THE BROOKLYN, OR NOT QUITE A MANHATTAN

SERVES 1

At one point in New York's history, Brooklyn was a well-to-do city, growing quickly and putting its own mark on the world. But then that upstart Manhattan and the combining of the boroughs seemed to relegate Brooklyn to the butt of many jokes. This drink's for you, all you folks out there in Brooklyn with your great arts, farmers' markets, and real neighborhoods. No, it's not quite a Manhattan—it might actually be better.

ICE CUBES
3 OUNCES YOUR FAVORITE HIGH-QUALITY BOURBON, SUCH AS
    BLANTON'S, VAN WINKLE, BASIL HAYDEN, OR EVEN GENTLEMAN JACK
    TENNESSEE WHISKEY
2 OR 3 DASHES PEYCHAUD'S BITTERS

1 Fill a cocktail shaker halfway full with ice cubes. Add the bourbon and the bitters. Shake vigorously until the drink is cold and sweat forms on the shaker. Let stand for 30 seconds.

2 Strain into a cocktail glass. Like Brooklyn, this drink needs no garnish.

THE BOURBON "ORANGE THING"

SERVES 1

This is a nod to Frank Stitt, chef and owner of Highlands Restaurant, Chez Fonfon, and Bodega in Birmingham, Alabama. Frank is considered one of the best chefs in the country and has been nominated for that award by the James Beard Foundation. He has also won the James Beard award for Best Chef South. His food is incredible; he uses French technique and local farm products. Don't even think about going to Birmingham without stopping at one of his establishments. A popular signature cocktail at his restaurants is "The Orange Thing." This is my bourbon salute to that cocktail and to Frank Stitt.

ICE CUBES
1½ OUNCES BOURBON
1½ OUNCES ORANGE LIQUEUR, SUCH AS GRAND MARNIER,
   COINTREAU, OR TRIPLE SEC
½ OUNCE VANILLA-FLAVORED VODKA OR VANILLA EXTRACT
½ OUNCE CLEAR CRÈME DE MENTHE
1 ORANGE TWIST, FOR GARNISH

1 Fill a cocktail shaker halfway full with ice cubes. Pour the bourbon, orange liqueur, vanilla vodka, and crème de menthe into the shaker. Shake vigorously until well chilled.

2 Strain into an oversized cocktail glass, and garnish with the orange twist. Serve immediately.

BOURBON RUSSIAN

SERVES 1

I developed this drink just for me because I love bourbon and hazelnuts, and when you toss in a little chocolate flavor it becomes one of those simply great little sippers. I like this drink with a roaring fire in the early evening. For me, it just helps slow the world down.

ICE CUBES
2 OUNCES BOURBON
½ OUNCE WHITE CRÈME DE CACAO
½ OUNCE HAZELNUT-FLAVORED LIQUEUR
3 TO 4 OUNCES HEAVY CREAM OR HALF-AND-HALF (YOU CAN EVEN USE
    2 PERCENT MILK IN A PINCH)
CHOCOLATE SHAVINGS FOR GARNISH

1 Fill a large cocktail shaker halfway full with ice cubes. Pour the bourbon, crème de cacao, hazelnut liqueur, and cream into the shaker. Shake vigorously until the drink is chilled.

2 Strain into an old-fashioned glass or pour the mixture, ice cubes and all, into a Collins glass. Garnish your prize with chocolate shavings, and enjoy.

MANGO BOURBON SLING

SERVES 2

Simply put, the Caribbean meets Kentucky. Or Tennessee. The mango, with its peach-like intent, coupled with the spice of the gingerroot pops the bourbon into a refreshing and slightly different concoction category. Perfect for a hot summer day.

1 TABLESPOON SUGAR
1 LEMON WEDGE (OPTIONAL)
ICE CUBES
4 MANGOS, PEELED AND FINELY DICED
1 TABLESPOON FINELY CHOPPED FRESH GINGER
4 OUNCES BOURBON
4 OUNCES GINGER ALE
FRESH MINT LEAVES FOR GARNISH

1 Pour the sugar onto a plate. Moisten the rims of 2 oversized cocktail or old-fashioned glasses with water or by running a lemon wedge around the top of the glass. Press the glasses into the sugar to rim the glass. Set aside.

2 Fill a large cocktail shaker halfway full with ice cubes. Add the mango, ginger, and bourbon to the shaker. Shake vigorously until the mixture is nicely chilled. Divide the mixture equally between the glasses, and float half the ginger ale on top of each drink. Garnish with mint leaves, and serve immediately.

BOURBON BOG

What makes this cranberry and bourbon concoction different from others is the inclusion of a sour mix and orange bitters. Those two ingredients play against the bourbon and cranberry juice to add some excitement and freshness to this drink.

ICE CUBES
1½ OUNCES BOURBON
1½ OUNCES CRANBERRY JUICE
2 TEASPOONS SOUR MIX (PAGE 19)
3 DASHES ORANGE BITTERS
FRESH CRANBERRIES OR MINT FOR GARNISH (OPTIONAL)

1 Fill a cocktail shaker with ice cubes. Add the bourbon, cranberry juice, sour mix, and bitters. Shake vigorously until the shaker is frosted.

2 Strain into a cocktail glass, garnish with cranberries or mint, if desired, and serve.

UMBRIAN MANHATTAN

SERVES 4

The Umbria region of Italy reminds me a bit of the hills where Jack Daniel's is distilled. On a recent trip to the region, I had had so much wine that I thought I was going to turn into a grape. My taste buds kept calling for Tennessee whiskey. A trip to the local co-op snagged a bottle of Jack Daniel's, which I drank with local water. Upon returning to the United States I decided to play around and see if I could come up with an Italian-style cocktail. Here's the result, and it's pretty doggone good.

ICE CUBES
4 ORANGE SLICES
8 MARASCHINO CHERRIES
8 OUNCES TENNESSEE WHISKEY
4 OUNCES DRY VERMOUTH
2 OUNCES CAMPARI
1 TABLESPOON SUPERFINE SUGAR

1 Fill 4 old-fashioned or highball glasses about halfway full with ice cubes. Squeeze an orange slice into each glass and drop the slice in the glass. Add a couple of maraschino cherries to each glass.

2 Add the whiskey, vermouth, Campari, and sugar to a cocktail shaker. Shake vigorously until the sugar is dissolved. Divide the mixture equally among the glasses and serve immediately.

COMMANDER'S PALACE INCREDIBLE MILK PUNCH

SERVES 4

New Orleans's famous Commander's Palace is home to one of the finest brunches in the country. They have two wonderful brunch cocktails. One is their spicy and peppery Bloody Mary, and the other is this soothing and rich milk punch. Also know that this milk punch is a perfect cure for a night of overindulgence. My friend Perry Batten introduced me to this beverage twenty-something years ago. It was his favorite way to start a Saturday morning. He claims that he got the recipe from Commander's Palace and, after visiting the restaurant and consuming several milk punches in the name of research, I'm convinced he had the real thing. So enjoy a trip to New Orleans without the plane fare.

1½ CUPS MILK
½ CUP HEAVY CREAM
12 OUNCES BOURBON
1 EGG WHITE
½ CUP SUPERFINE SUGAR
½ CUP VERY COLD WATER
1 TABLESPOON VANILLA EXTRACT
FRESHLY GRATED NUTMEG FOR GARNISH

Combine the milk, cream, bourbon, egg white, sugar, water, and vanilla in a container with a tight-fitting lid. Shake vigorously for a minute or two, and then divide among 4 old-fashioned glasses. Dust each with some nutmeg and serve.

> **NOTES:** Be sure to use a very fresh egg, and do not serve this drink to anyone with a compromised immune system.
> If you haven't brought whole nutmeg into your home yet, here's your excuse. Freshly grated nutmeg has a completely different taste from the ground nutmeg you buy in the spice section. It's easily shaved with a Microplane grater or on the smallest holes of a box grater. Even a special nutmeg grater is inexpensive.

NATCHEZ BELLE

SERVES 1

Natchez, Mississippi, may be one of the last bastions of the Old South. Fried chicken and deviled eggs abound, along with what I think is the South's most infamous side dish, tomato aspic. That said, they certainly know how to fix a bourbon cocktail there, and I have had many variations of these throughout the city. They're refreshing and not too strong, perfect for any Southern belle or New York woman.

> ICE CUBES
> 2 OUNCES BOURBON
> 2 OUNCES FRESHLY SQUEEZED ORANGE JUICE (FROM ABOUT ½ ORANGE)
> 2 OUNCES LEMON-LIME SODA
> 1 TEASPOON GRENADINE
> 1 FRESH MINT SPRIG

Fill a cocktail shaker halfway full with ice cubes and add the bourbon, orange juice, soda, grenadine, and mint sprig. Stir thoroughly to combine, mashing on the mint sprig as you stir. Pour into a highball glass and serve immediately.

PIPING HOT AND ICY

Bourbon can play in any temperature range. It likes to immerse itself in heat when the rest of the world is cold, and wrap an icy blanket around its golden hue when the temperature soars.

Bourbon, coffee, and chocolate, all with their individual hints of vanilla, like to be in a hot tub together. The spiciness that lurks behind most bourbons is a very pleasant note when the warmth hits it. Remember that bourbon is great sipping whiskey and nothing beats a warm fire, somebody to snuggle with, and some warm concoction laced with bourbon. It's almost a legal aphrodisiac.

At the opposite end of bourbon's temperature pole, when put into a frozen or semi-frozen state, bourbon becomes a party animal. While not knocking those clear-liquor icy cocktails, bourbon has depth and can take the cold without losing much flavor. My best summer evenings are spent with a Beach Bourbon Slush in hand while tending to the grill, watching the fire lightly char the food just as a good cooper chars a new bourbon barrel.

Hot or cold, bourbon has the ability to make your good moments better. Try all these recipes for the sheer fun of experimentation. You won't be sorry.

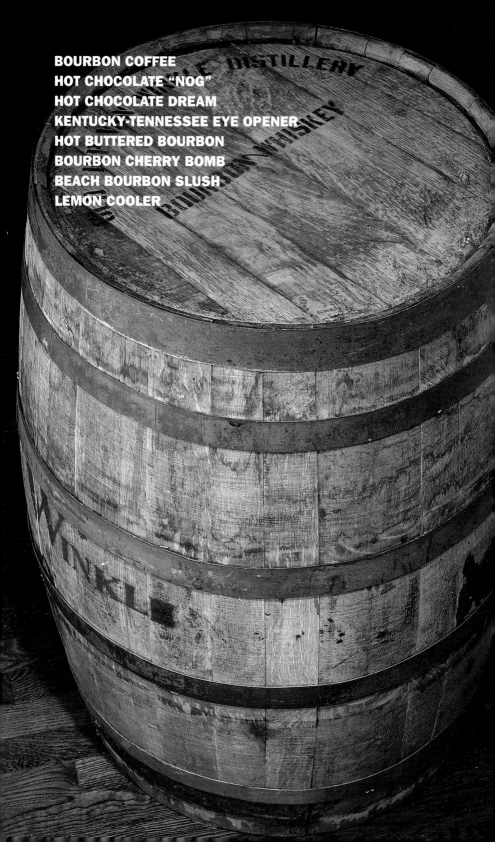

BOURBON COFFEE
HOT CHOCOLATE "NOG"
HOT CHOCOLATE DREAM
KENTUCKY-TENNESSEE EYE OPENER
HOT BUTTERED BOURBON
BOURBON CHERRY BOMB
BEACH BOURBON SLUSH
LEMON COOLER

BOURBON COFFEE

SERVES 4

The classic after-dinner coffee made with Irish whiskey takes on a new twist with the inclusion of bourbon. I find the smokiness that's inherent in bourbon adds to the flavor of the coffee and makes this generally a more enjoyable beverage than the classic.

24 OUNCES FRESHLY BREWED COFFEE
8 OUNCES BOURBON
4 OUNCES WHITE CRÈME DE MENTHE
1 TABLESPOON SUGAR
1 CUP WHIPPED CREAM
FRESH MINT LEAVES FOR GARNISH

Pour the coffee into a large carafe (or leave it in the pot if it's big enough). Stir the bourbon, crème de menthe, and sugar into the coffee. Divide the coffee mixture among 4 Irish coffee or regular mugs. Top each with whipped cream, and garnish with mint leaves. Serve immediately.

HOT CHOCOLATE "NOG"

SERVES 8

For a fun twist on a festive beverage, add some chocolate and bourbon to your eggnog. You could leave the bourbon out for the kids, but most of the merrymakers will want the "nog."

- 1 QUART EGGNOG
- 2 CUPS WHOLE MILK
- ½ CUP CHOCOLATE SYRUP
- 1 CUP BOURBON
- ¼ TEASPOON FRESHLY GRATED NUTMEG, PLUS MORE FOR GARNISH (OPTIONAL)

Pour the eggnog, milk, and chocolate syrup in a medium-size saucepan and place over medium heat. Heat almost to a boil, stirring constantly. Remove from the heat, and stir in the bourbon and nutmeg. Ladle into mugs. Sprinkle with additional nutmeg if desired, and serve immediately.

HOT CHOCOLATE DREAM

SERVES 4 TO 6

A hot chocolate made with peppermint patties would be decadent enough, but add some bourbon and you'll have a winner of a winter beverage. Light the fireplace.

- 2 CUPS HALF-AND-HALF
- 12 MINI PEPPERMINT PATTY CANDIES, CHOPPED
- 2 TABLESPOONS ARROWROOT
- 4 OUNCES BOURBON, OR MORE TO TASTE
- 4 TO 6 FRESH MINT SPRIGS, FOR GARNISH

1 Heat the half-and-half in a medium-size saucepan over medium heat until you begin to see bubbles along the side. Reduce the heat. Add the peppermint patties and whisk until melted and smooth.

2 Whisk in the arrowroot and allow the mixture to cook and thicken for a few minutes. Remove from the heat and stir in the bourbon. Divide among mugs, and garnish with mint sprigs. Serve immediately.

KENTUCKY-TENNESSEE EYE OPENER

SERVES 1

Technically this is a room-temperature drink, not a hot one, but since it involves coffee I decided to put it here with hot drinks. Everybody gets to play in this drink—both bourbon and Tennessee whiskey. We'll throw in some coffee and that other Southern syrup, molasses, to make a pretty fine middle-of-the-morning drink. Or if you top it with cream, it's almost a dessert.

> 1½ OUNCES JACK DANIEL'S OR OTHER TENNESSEE WHISKEY
> 1 TABLESPOON MOLASSES
> 1 TABLESPOON LIGHT BROWN SUGAR, PLUS ADDITIONAL FOR
>   SPRINKLING (OPTIONAL)
> 1 TEASPOON INSTANT ESPRESSO POWDER (REGULAR INSTANT COFFEE
>   WILL WORK IN A PINCH)
> 1½ OUNCES BOURBON

Add the Jack Daniel's to a small Mason jar, along with the molasses, brown sugar, and espresso powder. Place the lid on the jar and shake to combine. Add the bourbon, cover, and shake once again. If desired, sprinkle additional brown sugar over the top of the drink. Serve immediately or anytime within the next hour.

NOTE: If you would like to serve this as an after-dinner drink, add 1 to 2 ounces cream or half-and-half to the drink and shake one more time. Serve with a chocolate chip cookie and it's sure to put you into dreamland.

HOT BUTTERED BOURBON

SERVES 20

While we've all heard of hot buttered rum, and most of us have managed to have at least one during the cold winter months, I find that bourbon heightens the flavor and gives this classic drink a mellowing goodness. I've given you this recipe in a party quantity, and it even has a couple of make-ahead steps. So for Christmas, New Year's, or just-because-it's-January parties, give this one a try.

2 CUPS (4 STICKS) UNSALTED BUTTER, SOFTENED
1 POUND LIGHT BROWN SUGAR
1 POUND CONFECTIONERS' SUGAR
1 TABLESPOON GROUND CINNAMON
1 TABLESPOON FRESHLY GRATED NUTMEG
1 QUART HIGH-QUALITY VANILLA ICE CREAM, SOFTENED SLIGHTLY
ONE 750-MILLILITER BOTTLE BOURBON
4 QUARTS HOT BREWED COFFEE
20 CINNAMON STICKS, FOR GARNISH
1¼ CUPS WHIPPED CREAM, FOR GARNISH

1 Put the butter, brown sugar, confectioners' sugar, ground cinnamon, and nutmeg in a large bowl. With an electric mixer at medium speed, beat until light and fluffy, much as you would sugar and butter for baking. Stir in the ice cream. Pour the mixture into an airtight container and freeze until firm.

2 Combine the frozen ice cream mixture, bourbon, and hot coffee in a large punch bowl. Stir until the mixture begins to combine. Ladle into Irish coffee or regular mugs and serve. Have the cinnamon sticks and whipped cream available for folks to garnish their hot buttered bourbon.

> **NOTES:** If you like, you can keep the ice cream mixture on hand in the freezer for up to 2 months.
> To make just 1 serving of Hot Buttered Bourbon, combine 3 tablespoons of the ice cream mixture, 3 tablespoons bourbon, and ¾ cup hot coffee in a large mug. Stir until well combined. Garnish with a cinnamon stick and 1 tablespoon of the whipped cream.

BOURBON CHERRY BOMB

After watching Bobby Flay on one of his grilling shows make what he called a "bourbon cherry slushy," I thought his method of putting this together using a blender and making one drink at a time was not what I would want to do if I were having a summer party. So I came up with the following, which is prepared much like Beach Bourbon Slush (opposite page) and is a whole heck of a lot easier to serve to a crowd.

1 CUP WATER
ONE 12-OUNCE CAN FROZEN ORANGE JUICE CONCENTRATE, THAWED
ONE 12-OUNCE CAN FROZEN LEMONADE CONCENTRATE, THAWED
2 CUPS UNSWEETENED CHERRY JUICE
2 CUPS BOURBON
1 LITER LEMON-LIME SODA

1 In a 9 by 13-inch baking pan (preferably metal), stir together the water, the 2 concentrates, the cherry juice, and the bourbon. Put in the freezer and for the first couple of hours, stir the mixture with a fork every 15 to 20 minutes. Then leave in the freezer, covered, at least overnight to freeze thoroughly.

2 To prepare the drink, use an ice cream scoop or large spoon to put 2 scoops of the frozen mixture into an old-fashioned glass. Pour ¼ cup lemon-lime soda over the mixture and let sit for a few minutes before serving.

BEACH BOURBON SLUSH

SERVES AT LEAST 6, DEPENDING ON THIRST

I've just arrived at the beach, and is the first thing I do go check out the ocean? Heck, no. I start the process of making this concoction. No beach trip would be complete for me without it. Beach Bourbon Slush is great for any summertime event, and it has made a few trips as a tailgate beverage as well. It is also one of my most requested recipes. If you have a local hand-crafted ginger ale, use it for a burst of ginger through this drink.

2 CUPS UNSWEETENED BREWED BLACK TEA
5 CUPS WATER
1 PINT MAKER'S MARK BOURBON OR JACK DANIEL'S OLD NO. 7 WHISKEY
¼ CUP SUGAR
ONE 12-OUNCE CAN FROZEN LEMONADE CONCENTRATE, THAWED
ONE 6-OUNCE CAN FROZEN ORANGE JUICE CONCENTRATE, THAWED
CHILLED GINGER ALE AS NEEDED

1 In a large metal bowl (that will fit in your freezer), combine all of the ingredients except for the ginger ale. Place the bowl in the freezer, and every couple of hours or so, stir the mixture, until frozen.

2 To serve, use an ice cream scoop or a large, heavy spoon to fill an old-fashioned glass two-thirds full with the frozen tea mixture. Top with some ginger ale. Do not stir. Let the ginger ale coagulate with the frozen tea and make it all slushy, and then drink up.

LEMON COOLER

SERVES 4

This cocktail has the genetic makeup of a mint julep with a huge twist of lemon sorbet. This is a definite summer splurge when the three Hs—heat, humidity, and haze—take over your world.

8 FRESH MINT SPRIGS
2 TEASPOONS SUPERFINE SUGAR
8 OUNCES BOURBON
1 PINT LEMON SORBET
8 OUNCES CLUB SODA
ICE CUBES OR CRACKED ICE (OPTIONAL)

1 Place 2 mint sprigs and ½ teaspoon sugar in each of 4 old-fashioned glasses. Muddle until the mint is well bruised and crushed.

2 Divide the bourbon among the glasses. Add 2 scoops of the lemon sorbet to each glass. Top with club soda and serve, adding ice if desired.

BOURBON FOR A CROWD

Bourbon really likes a good party, and it especially likes the holidays. Punches, teas, and nogs based on bourbon are an unexpected turn of cocktail events. They are, however, welcome and refreshing and a memorable change of pace. All the recipes in this chapter can be scaled up or down easily, giving you the freedom to use them on occasions from a simple dinner party to a holiday open house. There is a good balance here of drinks for different seasons, and most all will taste just fine made without the spirits for the children and non-drinkers in the crowd.

Be responsible to your guests and your neighbors. Make sure that everyone can drive home without worry. Part of being a good host or hostess is also being a caring friend.

And here's a party tip: Instead of playing bartender all through the party, buy three or four large (at least 2-quart) pitchers—plastic double-walled ones are best—and make large batches of two or three of your favorites. Set the pitchers out on a buffet table, label them, and surround each with the appropriate glassware and garnishes. Just keep an eye on the level in the pitchers and refill when needed.

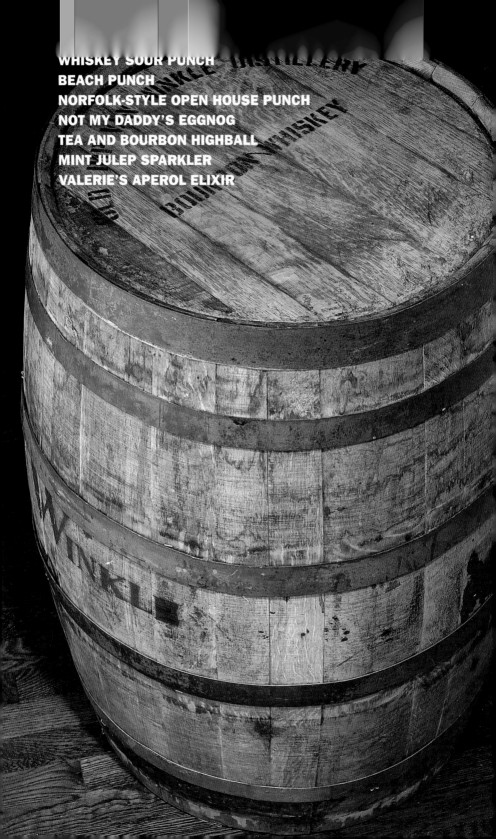

WHISKEY SOUR PUNCH
BEACH PUNCH
NORFOLK-STYLE OPEN HOUSE PUNCH
NOT MY DADDY'S EGGNOG
TEA AND BOURBON HIGHBALL
MINT JULEP SPARKLER
VALERIE'S APEROL ELIXIR

WHISKEY SOUR PUNCH

SERVES 25

Here's a way to take a classic whiskey sour and make it in volume, which will allow you to enjoy and join in with your own party.

2 QUARTS BOURBON
SIX 6-OUNCE CANS FROZEN LEMONADE CONCENTRATE, THAWED
THREE 6-OUNCE CANS FROZEN ORANGE JUICE CONCENTRATE, THAWED
THREE 6-OUNCE CANS FROZEN UNSWEETENED LEMON JUICE, THAWED
3 CUPS WATER
ICE CUBES

1 Combine all the ingredients in a punch bowl or 2-gallon container. Stir to combine, and refrigerate.

2 When ready to serve, place the bowl on your serving table with a ladle and punch cups. Have an ice bucket filled with ice handy for those who might enjoy additional chilling.

BEACH PUNCH

SERVES 8

Here's a quick punch to throw together for a party along the coast, or in your own backyard for that matter. The pineapple juice and ginger ale blend nicely with the sweetness of the bourbon for a refreshing afternoon cocktail. This also would be nice served at a bridge club or a ladies' luncheon. It doubles easily.

12 OUNCES FRESH PINEAPPLE JUICE
1 LITER GINGER ALE
8 OUNCES BOURBON
3 CUPS MIXED SEASONAL FRUIT, SUCH AS STRAWBERRIES, BLUEBERRIES,
    PINEAPPLE, OR PEACHES, CUT INTO BITE-SIZE PIECES
ICE CUBES

1 Combine the pineapple juice, ginger ale, and bourbon in a 2-quart or larger pitcher. Add the fruit and stir. Refrigerate until well chilled, at least 4 hours; overnight is even better.

2 When ready to serve, fill old-fashioned glasses about halfway full with ice cubes and pour the punch over. Serve immediately.

NORFOLK-STYLE OPEN HOUSE PUNCH

SERVES 36

Sometimes in all this battling between Kentucky bourbon and Tennessee whiskey, we forget that the Virginians have a true love of bourbon as well. This recipe came from a hostess from the Tidewater region of the state and is excellent as a spring or early summer punch for bridesmaid luncheons and graduations.

ONE 750-MILLILITER BOTTLE SOUTHERN COMFORT
6 OUNCES FRESHLY SQUEEZED LEMON JUICE (FROM 4 TO 6 LEMONS)
ONE 6-OUNCE CAN FROZEN ORANGE JUICE CONCENTRATE, THAWED
ONE 6-OUNCE CAN FROZEN LEMONADE CONCENTRATE, THAWED
3 LITERS LEMON-LIME SODA
2 CUPS ICE CUBES
5 LEMON SLICES
5 ORANGE SLICES

1 In a large punch bowl or other container, stir together the Southern Comfort, lemon juice, and 2 concentrates. Slowly pour in the lemon-lime soda. Refrigerate for at least 2 hours.

2 When ready to serve, place the bowl on your serving table and add the ice cubes. Add the lemon and orange slices. Let everyone serve themselves in punch cups, and you enjoy the party as well.

NOTE: Six-ounce cans of frozen concentrates can be hard to find in some areas of the country. If you can find only 12-ounce cans, buy them and simply use half of each when making this drink. "But, Fred," you ask, "what will I do with the rest of it?" Mix the 2 leftover concentrates together in a pitcher and add 1 liter lemon-lime soda. Stir to combine. There's always a child or a teetotaler around to appreciate this effort.

NOT MY DADDY'S EGGNOG

SERVES 20 TO 25

One of the mysteries of my childhood was the eggnog making that went on behind closed doors at my grandmother's house in rural North Carolina on Christmas Day. I later learned that a little moonshine and bourbon went into that nog, and that's probably why the adults were so happy when we got around to opening the presents. When the recipe was finally passed on to me and I realized how many raw eggs went into it, I decided I needed a different method. The answer came in the form of pasteurized eggs, which are now sold in most supermarkets. They are a little more expensive, but in situations where a recipe calls for raw eggs, they are a safe alternative. This still is a very old-fashioned eggnog, and every Christmas when I make it, I think of the joy that I had at my grandmother's house.

> 12 PASTEURIZED EGGS, SEPARATED
> 1 CUP SUGAR
> 8 OUNCES BOURBON
> 8 OUNCES APPLEJACK BRANDY
> ½ TEASPOON KOSHER SALT
> 6 CUPS HEAVY CREAM
> FRESHLY GRATED NUTMEG FOR GARNISH

1 Using an electric mixer, beat the egg yolks with the sugar until thick and very yellow. Add the bourbon and brandy slowly, stirring them into the yolk mixture. Cover and refrigerate for at least 2 or 3 hours.

2 Just before removing the yolk mixture from the fridge, beat the egg whites with the salt until stiff. Using clean beaters, whip the cream to soft peaks. Combine the egg whites and whipped cream into the yolk mixture by gently but quickly folding the mixtures together. Refrigerate for at least another hour or up to 4 hours.

3 Ladle the mixture into old-fashioned glasses and give each a grating of fresh nutmeg.

TEA AND BOURBON HIGHBALL

SERVES 8

I love combining tea and bourbon, especially when there are notes of orange and mint. This is a perfect party cocktail—allowing you to make it ahead and serve it with fanfare but without much effort. The recipe easily doubles.

1½ QUARTS BREWED BLACK TEA
ZEST OF 2 ORANGES
16 OUNCES MINT SIMPLE SYRUP (SEE NOTE)
16 OUNCES SINGLE-BARREL BOURBON
ICE CUBES
8 FRESH MINT SPRIGS, FOR GARNISH

1 In a large pitcher, combine the tea, orange zest, simple syrup, and bourbon. Cover and refrigerate overnight.

2 To serve, fill highball glasses with ice cubes and pour the bourbon-tea mixture into each glass. Garnish with mint sprigs, and serve.

NOTE: To make mint simple syrup, follow the directions for Simple Syrup (page 18), but add 1 bunch mint (about 3 ounces) to the sugar and water and discard the mint after the syrup has cooled.

MINT JULEP SPARKLER

SERVES 6

Here's a party twist on the mint julep. This drink has all the potency of a traditional julep, but with the added Champagne, the effervescence is refreshing. No need for those silver-plated julep cups, just good Champagne flutes.

¾ CUP LOOSELY PACKED FRESH MINT LEAVES
1 TABLESPOON SUPERFINE SUGAR
4 OUNCES BOURBON
ONE 750-MILLILITER BOTTLE VERY COLD CHAMPAGNE

1 In a small bowl, combine the mint leaves, sugar, and bourbon. Crush this mixture slightly to extract flavor from the mint. Cover the bowl and refrigerate for at least 6 hours; overnight is much better. The flavor continues to improve the longer the mixture is left to marry.

2 Remove the bourbon mixture from the refrigerator, and strain through a fine-mesh strainer into a bowl, pressing hard on the mint leaves to extract every bit of juice you possibly can. Discard the leaves.

3 Spoon 2 teaspoons of the bourbon-mint syrup into each of six Champagne flutes. (You'll have enough syrup left over to make another batch.) Equally divide the Champagne among the flutes, and serve immediately.

NOTE: The presentation and flavor of this drink is much more impressive when the Champagne flutes have been placed in the freezer for several hours.

VALERIE'S APEROL ELIXIR

SERVES 8

This recipe is the editor's choice, or at least proof to me that she had fun editing this book. Valerie Cimino, who hails from the Boston area, passed this recipe along to me after a successful run at one of her parties. She tells me the recipe actually calls for Scotch but she went with the top-shelf bourbon Knob Creek. I have used Tennessee whiskey, too, and both are good. Valerie says that she took some ribbing over the strength of the drink but that there was no problem with it disappearing. Hey, this lady edits cookbooks—it's got to be good, right?

16 OUNCES BOURBON
8 OUNCES SWEET VERMOUTH
8 OUNCES APEROL
ICE CUBES

1 Pour the bourbon, vermouth, and Aperol into a large pitcher. Add some ice cubes and stir to combine.

2 Fill old-fashioned glasses with more ice cubes and pour the mixture over the ice. Alternatively, if you have a large cocktail shaker, make it in that, and strain into cocktail glasses.

NOTE: Aperol is an Italian *aperitivo* created in 1919 by the Barbieri company, based in Padua, and it is now produced by the Campari company. Its ingredients include bitter orange, gentian, rhubarb, and cinchona.

EDIBLE BOURBON

Bourbon and Tennessee whiskey are not only a delight to drink, but also a right fair cooking ingredient. The spirit shows up in many recipes from the South and lower Midwest, and it takes well to both savory and sweet repasts. The purpose of this chapter is to give you just a taste of how bourbon works in food. Since the main purpose of this book is to introduce you to and add to your further enjoyment of America's whiskies, I've included only five recipes, two savory and three sweet. These recipes represent both classic and new thinking about using bourbon as a food ingredient, and I hope that you will use them as a springboard for other kitchen endeavors. Bourbon and Tennessee whiskey's sweet and smoky flavor profile, with hints of vanilla, caramel, and cloves, can add volumes to fall dishes such as pumpkin, sweet potatoes, and winter squash. Pork and poultry are also receptive to bourbon's essence. Bread puddings and pies with chocolate come alive with the presence of the spirit. Look to any Southern cookbook for ideas and more recipes.

BOURBON BRINE FOR TURKEY OR CHICKEN
SALMON WITH BROWN SUGAR AND BOURBON GLAZE
FRED'S BOURBON BALLS
THAT HORSE RACE PIE
MINT JULEP SORBET

BOURBON BRINE FOR TURKEY OR CHICKEN

MAKES ENOUGH FOR A 14- TO 16-POUND TURKEY

This brine will keep your poultry nice and moist as you cook it, especially when you're smoking it on the grill. The sweet natural smokiness of bourbon highlights and contributes to the flavors that rise from the fire. You can cut the recipe in half to do whole chickens. If you want some dynamite barbecued chicken, use this brine on chicken parts and taste what happens when the brine and barbecue sauce blend at the table.

2 CUPS KOSHER SALT
2 POUNDS LIGHT BROWN SUGAR
1½ CUPS BOURBON
1 GALLON ICE WATER
¼ CUP WHOLE CLOVES
¼ CUP WHOLE BLACK PEPPERCORNS

In a large plastic bag or container large enough to hold a turkey, combine the salt, sugar, bourbon, and water. The salt and sugar are not going to melt immediately; don't worry. Add the cloves and peppercorns. Put your turkey or chicken down into the brine and let sit, covered, in the refrigerator overnight. Drain and discard the marinade. Cook as you would poultry brined or marinated any other way.

SALMON WITH BROWN SUGAR AND BOURBON GLAZE

SERVES 4

This is an easy weeknight entrée that eats like it's the weekend. Simple to prepare, so keep the accoutrements simple as well—maybe a tossed salad and some long-grain and wild rice. This recipe will become one of your favorites with its sweet-sharp glaze flavors against the lush salmon.

¼ CUP (½ STICK) UNSALTED BUTTER
½ CUP PACKED DARK BROWN SUGAR
FOUR 6-OUNCE CENTER-CUT SALMON FILLETS (REMOVE ANY PIN BONES)
⅓ CUP BOURBON OR TENNESSEE WHISKEY

1 Melt the butter in a large, heavy skillet over medium heat. Stir in the brown sugar.

2 Place the salmon fillets, skin side up, on top of the brown sugar mixture. Cook for 5 minutes. Turn the salmon, and pour the bourbon around the fillets. Cook for 5 more minutes, or until the fish flakes easily with a fork. Serve, spooning the glaze over the salmon.

FRED'S BOURBON BALLS

MAKES ABOUT 36 BALLS

Bourbon balls used to be one of those little Christmas treats that were always around. I haven't seen them much lately, and until I started working on this book I had not made this recipe for several years. I should be ashamed of myself. Bourbon balls are a welcome addition to any assortment of cookies and candies around the holidays or as part of a dessert buffet. They're simple to make and have this sweet "burn" that's not quite like anything else.

2 CUPS CRUSHED VANILLA WAFER COOKIES
2 TABLESPOONS NATURAL COCOA POWDER
1½ CUPS CONFECTIONERS' SUGAR
1 CUP PECANS, FINELY CHOPPED
2 TABLESPOONS LIGHT CORN SYRUP
¼ CUP BOURBON

1 In a large bowl, mix together the vanilla wafer crumbs, cocoa, 1 cup of the confectioners' sugar, and the pecans. Add the corn syrup and bourbon. Mix well.

2 Shape the mixture into 1-inch balls, and roll each ball in the remaining ½ cup confectioners' sugar. Store in an airtight container for at least 12 hours before serving. Bourbon balls will keep, covered, for 4 to 5 weeks.

THAT HORSE RACE PIE

SERVES 8

"That horse race" is the Kentucky Derby, and this pie is a tradition for Derby Day parties. Can't call it a Derby Pie, though, because a bakery in Louisville gets real upset. This pie is too good for just one day. The chocolate, bourbon, and nuts just blend to perfection. It travels well, making it great for potlucks and family reunions. Make this pie often.

1 REFRIGERATED PIE CRUST FOR SINGLE-CRUST PIE OR YOUR OWN
   UNBAKED PIE CRUST
2 LARGE EGGS
½ CUP PLUS 1 TEASPOON GRANULATED SUGAR
½ CUP PACKED LIGHT BROWN SUGAR
½ CUP (1 STICK) UNSALTED BUTTER, MELTED AND COOLED
½ CUP ALL-PURPOSE FLOUR
1 CUP SEMISWEET CHOCOLATE CHIPS
1½ CUPS CHOPPED PECANS OR WALNUTS, TOASTED (I LIKE A MIX OF BOTH)
3 TABLESPOONS KENTUCKY BOURBON
1 CUP WHIPPING CREAM
1 TEASPOON PURE VANILLA EXTRACT

1 Preheat the oven to 350°F.

2 Place the pie crust in a 9-inch (not deep-dish) pie plate.

3 Beat the eggs, ½ cup of the granulated sugar, and the brown sugar in a large mixing bowl until well blended, about 1 minute. Add the butter and flour and continue beating until smooth. By hand, stir in the chocolate chips, nuts, and bourbon.

4 Pour into the pie crust. Bake for 35 to 40 minutes or until the top is brown. (A toothpick inserted will not be clean when removed but will be just not quite wet, similar to brownies.) Let cool on a rack.

5 Beat the cream with the remaining 1 teaspoon granulated sugar and the vanilla extract until it forms stiff peaks. Serve with the warm pie.

MINT JULEP SORBET

SERVES 4

Here's a mint julep in a whole different form that won't cause any arguments about how it's made, because it's just plain, flat good. Serve it in a traditional silver mint julep cup or a parfait glass that's been placed in the freezer and allowed to get frosty. Perfect for Derby Day or the sweltering heat of August.

1½ CUPS WATER
¾ CUP LIGHTLY PACKED FRESH MINT LEAVES, PREFERABLY SPEARMINT
  (ABOUT 2 SMALL BUNCHES)
½ CUP SUGAR
¼ CUP BOURBON
1 TABLESPOON GREEN CRÈME DE MENTHE
1 TEASPOON MINCED FRESH MINT LEAVES, PREFERABLY SPEARMINT
4 FRESH MINT SPRIGS, PREFERABLY SPEARMINT, FOR GARNISH

1 Combine the water, ¾ cup mint leaves, and sugar in a large saucepan. Place over medium heat and stir until the sugar dissolves. Raise the heat and slowly bring to a boil. Remove from the heat and pour into a medium-size bowl. Let cool to room temperature, and then cover and refrigerate for at least 2 hours.

2 Remove the mint syrup from the refrigerator and pass it through a fine-mesh strainer set over another bowl. Press down on the mint leaves to get them to release all of their flavor. Discard the mint leaves. Stir in the bourbon, crème de menthe, and minced mint leaves.

3 Process this mixture in your ice cream maker according to manufacturer's instructions. Transfer to a container, cover, and freeze until firm, about 2 hours. You can make this sorbet 2 to 3 days ahead. Scoop the sorbet into each of 4 cups, garnish with the mint sprigs, and serve immediately.

MEASUREMENT EQUIVALENTS

LIQUID CONVERSIONS

U.S.	METRIC
1 tsp	5 ml
1 tbs	15 ml
2 tbs	30 ml
3 tbs	45 ml
1/4 cup	60 ml
1/3 cup	75 ml
1/3 cup + 1 tbs	90 ml
1/3 cup + 2 tbs	100 ml
1/2 cup	120 ml
2/3 cup	150 ml
3/4 cup	180 ml
3/4 cup + 2 tbs	200 ml
1 cup	240 ml
1 cup + 2 tbs	275 ml
1 1/4 cups	300 ml
1 1/3 cups	325 ml
1 1/2 cups	350 ml
1 2/3 cups	375 ml
1 3/4 cups	400 ml
1 3/4 cups + 2 tbs	450 ml
2 cups (1 pint)	475 ml
2 1/2 cups	600 ml
3 cups	720 ml
4 cups (1 quart)	945 ml
	(1,000 ml is 1 liter)

WEIGHT CONVERSIONS

U.S.	METRIC
1/2 oz	14 g
1 oz	28 g
1 1/2 oz	43 g
2 oz	57 g
2 1/2 oz	71 g
3 oz	85 g
3 1/2 oz	100 g
4 oz	113 g
5 oz	142 g
6 oz	170 g
7 oz	200 g
8 oz	227 g
9 oz	255 g
10 oz	284 g
11 oz	312 g
12 oz	340 g
13 oz	368 g
14 oz	400 g
15 oz	425 g
1 lb	454 g

OVEN TEMPERATURE CONVERSIONS

°F	GAS MARK	°C
250	1/2	120
275	1	140
300	2	150
325	3	165
350	4	180
375	5	190
400	6	200
425	7	220
450	8	230
475	9	240
500	10	260
550	Broil	290

NOTE: All conversions are approximate.

INDEX

Note: Page references in *italics*
indicate photographs.

A

Algonquin, 32
Allegheny, 32, *33*
Aperol Elixir, Valerie's, 83
Apple, Washington, *48, 49*

B

Bar equipment, 13–15
Bar ingredients, 16–17
Bartending techniques, 15–16
Beach Punch, 76
Bitters, types of, 16
Blueberries
 Street Car, *44,* 45
Bluegrass Sunset, 43
Bourbon
 Balls, Fred's, *88,* 89
 Bog, 57
 Brine, for Turkey or Chicken, 86
 and Bubbly, 38, *39*
 Cherry Bomb, 70
 Coffee, 64
 Hot Buttered, *68,* 69
 "Orange Thing," The, 53
 Russian, 54, *55*
 Sazerac, 26
 Sling, Mango, 56
 Slush, Beach, 71
 Sour, 31
Bourbon, about
 compared to Tennessee Whiskey,
  9–10
 history, 6–8
 single barrel, 11
 small-batch, 10–11
 U.S. Congress definition, 9
Brandy
 Not My Daddy's Eggnog, *78, 79*
 Slap and Tickle, *46, 47*
Brine, Bourbon, for Turkey or Chicken,
 86

The Brooklyn, or Not Quite a
 Manhattan, 52

C

Cajun Comfort, 34
Champagne
 Bourbon and Bubbly, 38, *39*
 Mint Julep Sparkler, 82
Chapel Hill, 34
Cherry Bomb, Bourbon, 70
Chocolate
 Fred's Bourbon Balls, *88,* 89
 Hot, Dream, 65
 Hot, "Nog," 65
 That Horse Race Pie, 90, *91*
Chris McMillian's Mint Julep, *28,* 29
Coffee
 Bourbon, 64
 Hot Buttered Bourbon, *68,* 69
 Kentucky-Tennessee Eye Opener,
  66, *67*
Commander's Palace Incredible Milk
 Punch, 60
Cranberry juice
 Bourbon Bog, 57
 Washington Apple, *48, 49*
Cream
 Bourbon Coffee, 64
 Bourbon Russian, 54, *55*
 Commander's Palace Incredible Milk
  Punch, 60
 Hot Chocolate Dream, 65
 Not My Daddy's Eggnog, *78, 79*
Crème de cacao
 Bourbon Russian, 54, *55*
Crème de menthe
 Bourbon Coffee, 64

E

Eggnog
 Hot Chocolate "Nog," 65
 Not My Daddy's, *78, 79*
Egg whites, pasteurized, about, 19
Eleven Madison Park's Honey and
 Cardamom Bourbon, 51

Eye Opener, Kentucky-Tennessee 66, 67

F

Fred's Bourbon Balls, *88,* 89
Fruit. *See also specific fruits*
    Beach Punch, 76

G

Glassware, 11–12
Greenbrier's Mint Julep, The, 27

H

Hazelnut liqueur
    Bourbon Russian, 54, *55*
Honey and Cardamom Bourbon, Eleven
    Madison Park's, 51
Hot Buttered Bourbon, *68,* 69
Hot Chocolate Dream, 65
Hot Chocolate "Nog," 65
Hot sauce, buying, 17

I

Ice, for cocktails, 17

K

Kentucky-Tennessee Eye Opener, 66, 67

L

Lemonade, Lynchburg, 50
Lemon juice
    Bourbon Sour, 31
    Cooler, 72, *73*
    Homemade Sour Mix, 19
    Norfolk-Style Open House Punch, 77
Lime juice
    Homemade Sour Mix, 19
    Scarlett O'Hara, 35

M

Mango Bourbon Sling, 56
Manhattan, 24
Manhattan, Perfect, 25
Manhattan, Umbrian, *58,* 59
Milk
    Hot Chocolate "Nog," 65
    Punch, Commander's Palace
    Incredible, 60

Mint
    Hot Chocolate Dream, 65
    Lemon Cooler, 72, *73*
    simple syrup, preparing, 80
    Tea and Bourbon Highball, 80, *81*
Mint Julep
    Chris McMillian's, *28,* 29
    The Greenbrier's, 27
    Sorbet, 92
    Sparkler, 82

N

Natchez Belle, 61
New Fashioned, 42
Norfolk-Style Open House Punch, 77
Not My Daddy's Eggnog, *78,* 79

O

Old Fashioned, 22, *23*
Orange juice
    Bluegrass Sunset, 43
    The Bourbon "Orange Thing," 53
    Natchez Belle, 61
    Norfolk-Style Open House Punch, 77
    Ward 8, 30

P

Peaches
    New Fashioned, 42
Pecans
    Fred's Bourbon Balls, *88,* 89
    That Horse Race Pie, 90, *91*
Perfect Manhattan, 25
Pie, That Horse Race, 90, *91*
Pineapple juice
    Beach Punch, 76
    Slap and Tickle, 46, *47*
Punches
    Beach Punch, 76
    Commander's Palace Incredible Milk
        Punch, 60
    Hot Buttered Bourbon, *68,* 69
    Norfolk-Style Open House Punch, 77
    Not My Daddy's Eggnog, *78,* 79
    Whiskey Sour Punch, 76

S

Salmon with Brown Sugar and Bourbon
    Glaze, 87

Sazerac, Bourbon, 26
Scarlett O'Hara, 35
Simple Syrup
  mint, preparing, 80
  from Scratch, 18
  Vanilla, 18
Slap and Tickle, 46, *47*
Sorbet, Mint Julep, 92
Sour Mix, Homemade, 19
Southern Comfort
  Cajun Comfort, 34
  Norfolk-Style Open House Punch, 77
  Scarlett O'Hara, 35
Southern Love, *36, 37*
Street Car, *44, 45*
Sugar, for cocktails, 17

T

Tea
  Beach Bourbon Slush, 71
  and Bourbon Highball, 80, *81*
Tennessee Whiskey
  compared with bourbon, 9–10
  Kentucky-Tennessee Eye Opener,
    66, 67
  Lynchburg Lemonade, 50

Umbrian Manhattan, *58,* 59
That Horse Race Pie, 90, *91*
Tools, bar, 13–15
Triple Sec
  The Bourbon "Orange Thing," 53
  Chapel Hill, 34
  Lynchburg Lemonade, 50

V

Valerie's Aperol Elixir, 83
Vanilla Simple Syrup, 18
Vermouth
  Algonquin, 32
  Allegheny, 32, *33*
  Manhattan, 24
  Perfect Manhattan, 25
  Umbrian Manhattan, *58,* 59
  Valerie's Aperol Elixir, 83
Vodka
  The Bourbon "Orange Thing," 53
  Slap and Tickle, 46, *47*

W

Ward 8, 30
Washington Apple, *48,* 49
Whiskey Sour Punch, 76

ABOUT THE AUTHOR

FRED THOMPSON is a food writer, a food stylist, and a culinary developer. He is the author of *Lemonade, Iced Tea, Crazy for Crab, Hot Chocolate, Barbecue Nation,* and *Grillin' with Gas.* He writes "The Weekend Gourmet" column for the *News and Observer* in Raleigh, North Carolina, and is the publisher of *Edible Piedmont* magazine. He also writes for *Fine Cooking* magazine, *Wine & Spirits,* and *Every Day with Rachael Ray* and is a popular cooking-school teacher. He lives in Raleigh and New York City.